A SUSSEX GUIDE

Welcome Home Demi —

hope you get to explore
Some of these over time.

love from

Amanda, Tom & Max

GOOD
FOOD & DRINK
IN SUSSEX

FIZZ CARR

INTRODUCED BY
DAVID DIMBLEBY

Illustrated by
JOANNA KERR

SNAKE RIVER PRESS

SNAKE RIVER PRESS

Book No 12
Books about Sussex for the enthusiast

Published in 2008 by
SNAKE RIVER PRESS
South Downs Way, Alfriston, Sussex BN26 5XW
www.snakeriverpress.co.uk

ISBN 978-1-906022-11-2

This book was conceived, designed and produced by
SNAKE RIVER PRESS

ART DIRECTOR & PUBLISHER *Peter Bridgewater*
EDITORIAL DIRECTOR *Viv Croot*
EDITOR *Rob Yarham*
PAGE MAKEUP *Richard Constable & Chris Morris*
ILLUSTRATOR *Joanna Kerr*
CONSULTANT *Lorraine Harrison*

This book is typeset in Perpetua & Gill Sans,
two fonts designed by Eric Gill

Printed and bound in China

DEDICATION

For Steve

CONTENTS

FOREWORD

Fizz Carr's erudite and witty study of food production in Sussex should be read by anyone interested in how our food is produced, not just in Sussex but anywhere. It explains through the vivid descriptions of local food producers the complexity of their work, and the degree to which they depend on climate, soil and the local culture.

It is commonplace to bemoan the bland, over-packaged food produced by so many supermarkets. But as any busy household knows, the convenience of supermarket food is a boon. It saves time shopping, is relatively cheap and usually guarantees a degree of quality. What it lacks is character. This springs from our attitude to food. We deceive ourselves if we think that a hundred years ago we ate better than we do today. For most people buying food produced locally imposed restrictions on their diet, restrictions imposed by the seasons and the harvest and local conditions. No-one except a few fanatics would want to go back to a world when the only food we ate was produced within twenty miles of our homes.

But what is also now increasingly understood is what we have lost by neglecting local food. The encouraging growth in farm shops and farmers' markets is restoring to our tables the variety and the quality of food which the supermarkets cannot provide. It takes more effort to find local suppliers and support them. But the effort is repaid, as Fizz Carr convincingly argues, by the greater subtlety of the food they sell and by knowing a little about how it is produced.

There is a lesson here for everyone who cares about what they eat, both those who are worried by the carbon footprint of strawberries flown in out of season from California, and those who simply want their table enriched by the taste of food produced on a small scale and with the welfare of the animals and the environment paramount.

Local food is not an easy option. It demands time and energy to find and it costs a little more but the rewards of including at least some local food in our diet are immense. In the rush of our increasingly complex lives it adds something that can so easily go missing: an attachment to the land and the culture of the country we live in and a willingness to relish its infinite variety. That is reward enough – to say nothing of the delicious flavours described here, which will set the taste buds tingling.

DAVID DIMBLEBY

INTRODUCTION

*'I shouldn't think even millionaires could eat anything
nicer than new bread and real butter and honey for tea.'*
DODIE SMITH, *I CAPTURE THE CASTLE, 1948*

Sixty years ago we were preserving every egg we could get our hands on, cooking every scrap of meat we were entitled to, gloating over every spoonful of sugar. As Virginia Woolf, living in Sussex during the war, wrote on being given some butter by a farming friend:

> *Then in the glory of my heart I gave all our week's ration — which is about the size of my thumb nail — to Louie then sat down and ate bread and butter. Think of our lunch tomorrow! In the middle of the table I shall put the whole pat. And I shall say: Eat as much as you like.*

It's hard to imagine anyone getting quite so excited about a lump of butter nowadays. Most of us can afford to buy the food that we feel like any day of the week. Most of us can eat meat daily if we choose to. We rarely queue for food and we throw away a sizeable percentage of the food that we buy rather than recycle it into leftovers. It's hard not to reach the conclusion that we have come to take our food for granted. And ironically, now that the vast majority of us can stop worrying about the daily problem of finding enough food to eat, we're perhaps more worried by our food than at any other time in our history. Is it safe, is it healthy, is it kind, is it cruel, is it sustainable? Truly, choice can be a confusing thing, particularly in Britain, to a society that, having industrialised so early, has lost touch with many of its rural roots.

Our concerns about climate change and food miles, our growing disillusionment with the taste of food that may have travelled thousands of miles, our worries about animal welfare — all these issues have started to renew our interest in local food once more. The difference, of course, is that we are usually exercising choice when we buy our food, in contrast to our elders who bought food locally because that's all there was. We're as likely now to visit high-profile farm shops and fashionable farmers' markets as castles and museums on our Sunday mornings. Provenance – a word that until recently sounded like it should only belong at a fine art auction – is now synonymous with the word 'local'.

And perhaps we are finally starting to realise that unless we champion our local food producers, unless we actively seek out and demand locally grown food, then our local food culture will disappear. The cost of food production today in the UK has never been higher. Expensive oil, expensive land and, above all, expensive labour mean our farmers and food producers are thrown into direct competition with farmers in less developed countries around the world with far lower costs who are now enjoying access to our market with reduced levels of import tariffs. While there will always be a need for imported food (unless we change our buying habits very drastically) most people would like to see a home-grown industry flourishing too.

Sourcing local food will mean that you will undoubtedly spend longer shopping and planning your shopping. It's hard to say whether you will spend more money or less – but there are many advantages to sourcing local food. First and foremost there is the welfare factor. It's reassuring to be able to see the chickens that lay your eggs, or to find out a little more about the bullock who's going to play a starring role in your eagerly planned *boeuf en daube*. It's pleasing to know that it has spent its entire life in the fields just five miles away before a quick ten-mile trip to the abattoir. It's also good to know that it's then had a full three weeks hanging in a cold store to develop its flavour.

The supermarkets have started to respond to the local issue slowly, slowly – highlighting small, specially chosen ranges of local foods. It's a start. But the supermarkets' centralised operations make selling regional food a real challenge for them. And the whole point of locally provenanced food becomes rather meaningless if that food has travelled, say, from a field near a store in Hailsham in Sussex, to the store's headquarters in central England for packaging and labelling, only to return again to Hailsham by lorry a few days later. It's frustrating that so much of the fish caught off our shores is rejected by our own superstores as being too varied in size to sell, which means it is all then sent off to supermarkets in the Netherlands who have a more enlightened approach to fish buying. As someone who would be happy to buy any size of Dover sole, I resent the disappearance across the Channel of so many of these delicious fish.

I write about the terrain of the county in pretty well every chapter of this book. Sussex has a little of the most productive, and a lot of the least productive, land in the country and this has had a huge effect on the types of farming that have always taken place. Our ancestors once relied on teams of oxen to plough their land. We may have powerful tractors now that can pull the most sophisticated ploughs and seed drills, but essentially the same kinds of farming still take place in the same places in the county. The triangle of flat alluvial that starts at Shoreham and stretches to Chichester in the west has always been of prime horti-cultural importance. The soil, the light, the mild climate – none of this has changed so very much in the past couple of hundred years. It's just that the scale of the industry is now that much more extraordinary. Once it was the cart that took produce from the area to other markets, then it was the fruit train and now it is the refrigerated lorry.

But good food and drink is as much about the skill and dedication of the people who produce it as it is about soil type and climate. Many of the people featured in this book work every day of the week. Their hours are often ridiculously long and unsociable – 5 to 9 as one grower rue-fully puts it, rather than 9 to 5. Their work is frequently dangerous, at times unpleasant, and often extremely dreary. Long days (or nights) of physical toil are usually followed by hours of necessary paperwork and bureaucracy – from animal movements to health and safety records.

So this book aims to tell you a little more about what these people do in order to get their produce to you. Even at farmers' markets and farm shops where we're perhaps a little better informed about the nature of our next meal, we very rarely consider the sheer effort of getting that meal to us. That plump chicken on the table has been raised from chick; fed, watered, checked for health every day for 80 days, then slaughtered, plucked, drawn and dressed, giblets bagged and inserted, chilled and then transported. Perhaps the producer then stands at a windy stall, open to the elements for a five-hour stretch. At a pound or two more than an intensively reared bird, is this chicken really expensive? The loaf of bread on the shelf at 8.30 am has kept a baker from his bed perhaps for two nights. The dough has been mixed, slowly fermented, shaped, set to rise once more, slashed with a blade, baked and cooled. Should we really be complaining that it costs us 50p more than a loaf rushed through an industrial process in less than two hours?

What motivates these people to produce our food? What makes a fisherman launch his boat into the surf from the beach on a spiteful February morning for a few crates of watery catch? What impulse drives a London couple to end lucrative City careers, sell their house, and risk everything on starting a chocolate shop?

For some it's simply that they have identified a demand for a particular product and their entrepreneurial spirit – perhaps honed in other industries – has given them the confidence to turn their hand to something else. For others it's an escape from an inner-city life and a desire to get in touch with the land. For some it's a philosophical need to serve their local community by producing food in a manner that they feel comfortable with – maybe organically, maybe bio-dynamically. And there are many who cannot imagine doing anything else other than produce food, in the same way as their forebears have done. They in turn expect the next generation to follow them on.

The odd recipe is dotted through the chapters but this book makes no claim to be a source of traditional Sussex fare. For that you should turn to the excellent *Sussex Recipe Book – with a Few Excursions into Kent* by M. K. Samuelson, which brings together a fascinating collection of dishes – recipes for 'sullibubs' and wheatear pies amongst them. (Wheatears are little lark-like birds that were once trapped by the Downland shepherds during the summer months, and sold for a penny a bird.) I reproduce one recipe from the *Sussex Recipe Book*, but the others are inspired by the conversations I have enjoyed with the producers I have met in the research for this book. And I hope that you, too, having read the book, are similarly inspired – both to support local producers and, wherever possible, include their produce in your cooking.

PART ONE

FISH & SEAFOOD

While the coastal population of the county has always relied on the sea for its fish, inland fish ponds – larders, in effect, for live freshwater fish – were once common features, particularly of the Wealden landscape. Many of these fish-ponds were 'furnace ponds', created by the damming of streams and rivers to provide power for the once-famed Sussex iron industry. When the iron industry moved to the northern industrial districts the ponds were later stocked with freshwater fish. Arthur Young records in 1812 that carp was the 'chief stock' of these fishponds, although 'tench and perch, eels and pike, are raised' too. Much of the fish was transported to London.

Nowadays we look almost exclusively to the sea for our fish and, more often than not, to the seas elsewhere – to the cod, haddock and plaice of the North Atlantic and, increasingly, even to the wealth of the Pacific. Much of the county's Channel sea catch seems to be more prized by consumers in France, Portugal and the Netherlands than it does here at home which seems an enormous shame. As one Sussex fisherman ruefully says, it seems that the British only eat fish when they go on holiday abroad.

THE SUSSEX DAY BOATS

SUSTAINABLE FISHING

The vast majority of Sussex fishing boats are day boats – small craft that hug the coastline or venture just a few miles out to sea. They might now have diesel engines, use motorised winches, have plastic nets and fish-tracking devices but in many ways they've hardly changed from the boats that were putting out to sea a hundred years ago. They're still small boats at the mercy of the winds and they still battle for survival in competition with the beam trawlers that sweep the seabeds of the Channel for days and sometimes weeks at a time. There is frustration that while small boats (under 33 ft or 10 metres) make up 93 per cent of the national fleet and 83 per cent of the workforce, yet they are allocated only 3 per cent of the national fish quota. And it's these bigger boats, the smaller fisheries claim, that are responsible for the depletion of certain fish stocks by their all-too-effective fishing methods. It's the very inefficiency of small-boat fishing methods that, after all, makes fishing sustainable.

Big iron steam trawlers started to replace the small wooden fishing boats across the country in the 19th century. But there was little impetus or will in Sussex to invest in the infrastucture like docks and handling facilities necessary to support these changes to the fishing fleet. Around 2000 people were living at Brighton in 1750 and half of these were people associated in some way or other with the fishing industry. By 1850, the number of fishermen remained the same but the general population of the town had swollen to 40,000. The movement of people to the county's coastal towns and villages and the growth in tourism meant that fishing and fishermen became increasingly sidelined and then positively unwelcome on the beach. Trawlers were landing huge quantities of fish into the large industrial ports elsewhere. For the first time it became cheaper to buy North Sea trawlered fish that had travelled halfway across the British Isles by train than to go down to the beach and buy it direct from a fisherman in his wooden Sussex boat.

Despite its lack of a natural harbour, Hastings has been an important fishing centre for well over a thousand years owing to its proximity to some of the country's most plentiful fishing grounds. Even before the Norman invasion, Hastings' connections with the French coast meant that it was one of the most important fishing centres in England. Hastings fishermen were at the forefront of the medieval herring industry, taking the lead in the founding of Yarmouth as the prime fishery port for herring. So great was their influence in Yarmouth that their property holdings and preferential rights caused extreme resentment among the Yarmouth locals, which resulted in a bloody battle in the late 13th century that left 17 Yarmouth vessels burnt and 165 men dead.

Hastings men were still fishing in the North Sea around Yarmouth and Lowestoft in the 19th century, the fleet made up of comparatively large boats called 'luggers'. These followed the shoals of mackerel along the Cornish coast in the summer and spent the autumn and winter months chasing herring in the North Sea.

But when the town started to develop as a desirable seaside destination for the wealthy, in the late 18th and early 19th centuries, its fashionable status spelled the beginning of an uneasy relationship between the fishing industry and the town's other business interests that was to continue for almost two centuries. With the fishermen ensconced on what is now the eastern side of the town, rapid new development to support a high-class tourist industry was forced westwards to the St Leonards area. The fashionable visitors soon melted away but with the establishment of a middle-class business district in this western part of town, the fishing industry became geographically and spiritually sidelined.

The conflict of fishing and business interests continued well into the next century. The growing popularity of the mass-tourism market meant that the fishing boats were jostling for position with boating lakes and amusement parks. Fishing was perceived by the town's leaders as a dying industry. The fish stocks had become heavily depleted, and it wasn't until 1964 when the fishing limits were extended from 3 to 12 miles

(5 to 15 km) – the inner 6 miles (10 km) being exclusive to Britain – that stocks started to recover.

A significant boost to the town's fishermen has been the fishery's gaining in 2005 of Marine Stewardship Council (MSC) certification for three of the species that make up an important share of its catch – mackerel, herring and Dover sole. The MSC is an independent global organisation that aims to set the gold standard for sustainable and well-managed fisheries.

Mackerel and herring are pelagic fish that are found in open seas and move seasonally through the local waters, rather like tourists. Herring are fished around Hastings between the end of November and the beginning of January. Mackerel are summer visitors, caught between April and September. Dover sole, by contrast, is a demersal fish, found near the sea bed. For this reason, it has a much larger fishing season between March to December. A particularly good source of Dover sole lies on the sea bed between Hastings and Dungeness and stocks are apparently plentiful. The sole are caught either with the selective trammel nets – which consist of three layers of netting very similar in shape to a tennis net – or with gill nets which are similar but consist of just one layer of netting. These nets are fixed – usually set in place on one tide, with the net hauled back in and the catch collected at the following tide. Damage to the sea bed is minimal, and by-catch – other, unwanted species – is lessened. It's significant that, unlike most of the other certified MSC fisheries, very few changes had to be made to Hastings' fishing practices in order to get MSC accreditation. So if you want to buy a delicious MSC Dover sole to cook for your supper, you'll have to make a trip to the Rock-a-Nore fishmonger on the Hastings Stade.

The MSC system does not just certify the fishing fleets. The system ensures that everybody involved in the fish's journey from sea to shop – the wholesaler, the fishmonger, the restaurant – must be properly checked and audited to ensure that good practice is followed every step of the way. Even the local bakery – Judge's Bakery in the High Street – has to receive Chain of Custody certification in order to sell their spiced mackerel and kipper 'Mack-a-Rolls' and 'Rock-a-Nore Rolls'.

A day in the life of a Newhaven fisherman

Mick Scott, a 'full-time' Newhaven fisherman for the past 32 years, started 'messing about with boats' when he was five. He fishes in a 'shared boat system' where the catch is shared out in a set ration between the crew and the boat and her net.

'In summer I'm up at 4 am, later in the winter – it's just a case of trying to make the most of the daylight. You develop a plan the night before – decide what kind of fishing you're going to do the next day. We fish everything. I've just finished a good session fishing squid and cuttlefish. Newhaven's renowned traditionally for its scallops but I don't fish them – I don't like the dredging. It's the sheer weight of the gear – over a ton and a half of stuff comes smack against the side of the boat and it's too easy to get hurt.

'I'll be out after bass over the next few days. You need nice, 'dirty' water for bass so that they don't see you coming and it's been rough the past couple of days so I haven't been out but they give a good weekend. I'll steam out for 10 minutes and then chuck out the net and go west. The net I use is a plain white fish net – about 240-ft- (73-m-) long – it's made of a much better-quality plastic than the old one and it saves me £20 in diesel each time I go out as it's much lighter to pull along.

'After a couple of hours, I'll haul in the net. That takes about 40 minutes. I'll empty out the fish into the boat and then the net goes back out. I sort out the good stuff – anything too small goes back, as does anything I don't have quota for. We gut the stuff we're keeping, wash it and put it on ice. We'll bring the nets in twice more, then turn for home. Sometimes the dolphins come and swim with us. They swim along in front, always in front as if they're leading us. Often they'll stay all day and they only leave us when we get to the harbour mouth.

'We unload the catch and put it in the fridge. I leave about 6 am so it's often a 14-hour day. The catch gets picked up by the van about 10 pm in the evening. They weigh and grade the fish but I think about 75 per cent of the catch probably goes to Boulogne – there's no market in this country.

'I'm restricted to three days fishing a week because my boat is over 33 ft (10 m) long – the other days it's maintenance, but I've also got a job with the Royal Mail. There's no fortune to made from fishing but it's what I do and I can't imagine doing anything else. I suppose if I sold the boat I could buy a few flats or something but I'm hanging in here for my son – I wish he were a bit older, really, so I could stop. My son will take the boat over and then he'll look after me. That's the way it works.'

OYSTERS & SHELLFISH

FROM STAPLES TO LUXURIES

It's extraordinary to think that only 200 years ago oysters were in such abundance that they were an absolute staple food for the very poorest people. 'It's a wery remarkable circumstance, sir', said Sam Weller in Dickens' *Pickwick Papers*, 'that poverty and oysters always seem to go together.' Stewed, cooked in pies, often used as little more than a condiment in boiled beefsteak puddings, they were a cheap, highly nutritious form of protein for the masses. A far cry, indeed, from the luxury oyster bars of today where a dozen of the now upmarket bivalves can easily cost you £25 a time.

Until the mid- to late 19th century, the Sussex coast was a particularly fertile source of shellfish. Shoreham fishermen dredged oysters from mid-Channel seabeds and then kept them alive in beds in the river. Oysters were sent all over the country – 18,000 tonnes (20,000 tons) went by railway from Shoreham alone at the height of the 19th-century trade – and when new oyster beds were discovered just outside Littlehampton, so many fishermen from around the country turned up to exploit the area that the boats had to be moored in the harbour three or four deep. The consequence of the over-fishing caused by this oyster gold rush, and the spread of disease that made the remaining shellfish unsafe to eat, was that by the 1860s the oyster industry was largely extinct in the county.

Still, shellfish of another sort are still very much harvested in the area. A higgledy-piggledy collection of pots and cages lines the promenade at Selsey's East Beach. The rocky seabed of this coastline provides a natural habitat for the crabs and lobsters that the town has long been famous for – Selsey fishermen once supplied shellfish to the *Queen Elizabeth* and *Queen Mary* luxury liners, where they were kept live on board in large tanks.

Catching crabs & lobsters

It's 1.30 pm on a sparkling August Friday and Keith Birkett has just brought ashore this morning's harvest. He pulls back a cover on one pot to reveal a mass of gently waving claws and antennae – brown crabs and lobsters, which at this time of year shimmer an iridescent purple. He puts his hand in and gently feels amongst the bony skeletons, gently turning his catch over for me and pointing out the finest specimens. He's been out at sea since 5 am. His furthest pots lie a full hour-and-a-half's chug from the boat's moorings in the sea in front of us. The sea in these waters can be amazingly shallow – at low tide he can go a full 5 miles (8 km) out to sea and still be in only 10 ft (3 m) depth of water.

The pots are arranged in strings, between 25 to 40 to a string. One by one, each pot is pulled aboard, the catch taken out and measured for size. (An escape hatch sewn into one side of each pot ensures that the very smallest shellfish don't end up as livebait for the larger specimens.) The bigger ones are kept, and the smaller ones put back in the sea to grow on. Then the pots are baited once more with strips of dead fish and tossed back into the water. Knowing where and when the lobsters are likely to be found is a skill that is learnt only by experience but, generally speaking, the best lobsters are found in-shore between May and June but in deeper water in July and August. Careful attention has to be paid to the positioning of pots in particular sorts of weather – in winter and when bad weather is forecast, the pots go out to deeper waters where they are less likely to be damaged. Lobsters usually moult their shells in the spring and autumn, weather permitting, retreating to their holes in the seabed. Once they've shed the shell, they eat it, waiting in their burrows in the rocks for their new shells to harden before once more venturing out to feed a few weeks later. Without their shells, Birkett says, they look 'like jelly'.

Since May 2007 Birkett has been selling part of his catch direct to the public, mainly at farmers' markets around the south-east. So rather than delivering most of his shellfish to the wholesaler next door (which will then be sent to be traded at Billingsgate fish market before heading off to a fish shop or restaurant and then to a customer) he has decided to cut out all of these middle men. Instead, he buys what he needs for the next day's market 'from his boat' (this is a Government obligation, to ensure traceability) and spends his afternoons cooking and preparing his fish for sale. Only very occasionally is he asked for live shellfish but he is happy to supply these with prior notice. Anxious not to tread on a like-minded colleague's toes, his only Sussex markets are at Haywards Heath and East Grinstead, and he concentrates on supplying mainly the Thames Valley network of farmers' markets concentrated around Surrey and Berkshire.

His big problem at the moment is keeping up with demand, he says, and he is applying for planning permission to extend his shed on the beach so that he has more room for chilling and processing. This aside, he does worry about the long-term future of the fishing industry at Selsey. He thinks that there are fewer lobsters about, and the stocks of brown crab are moving northwards to the cooler seas around Scotland, he says, leaving the warm Channel waters. There are plenty of spider crabs, prized by continental Europe for their sweet meat, but Birkett all but shudders when they're mentioned. 'Too ugly to eat', he says.

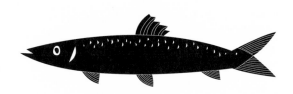

DOVER SOLE WITH SPINACH & NUTMEG CREAM SAUCE

A fish of such delicious flavour as the Dover sole needs only the simplest of cooking.

INGREDIENTS
SERVES 2

- Unsalted butter, 100 g
- 2 medium-sized Dover sole. Ask your fishmonger to skin one side
- Plain flour for coating
- Salt and pepper
- Cooking oil
- Fresh leaf spinach, a good handful
- Double cream, 175 ml
- Nutmeg to season

INSTRUCTIONS

1. Melt 75 g of unsalted butter in a saucepan, turn up the heat and boil the butter for just under a minute. Then switch off the heat and let the butter rest for 10 minutes before pouring it through a sieve lined with kitchen paper into a bowl. The white solids will stay trapped in the paper and you'll be left with golden buttery oil that won't burn as you fry the fish.

2. Cut any tough stalks out of the spinach leaves and wash them well. Shred the leaves into thin ribbons (easy if you roll up a few leaves together into a fat sausage first). Add the spinach to a pan of salted boiling water and blanch the leaves for just a minute if using young spinach (allow a couple of minutes more if it's more mature). Drain the spinach, press out as much water as possible and set to one side.

3. Shake some plain flour onto a plate, season it well with salt and pepper and coat both sides of the fish in the flour. Heat a couple of tablespoonfuls of oil in the frying pan. Shake off the excess flour and add the fish to the pan, frying over a medium heat for about five minutes each side.

4. While the fish is cooking, melt a knob of butter until it starts to foam and stir in the cooked spinach. Add the cream, season with salt, pepper and some grated nutmeg, and simmer for a couple of minutes until the sauce is slightly reduced and thickened. Taste for seasoning.

Serve with some boiled new or sauté potatoes.

PART TWO

MEAT & GAME

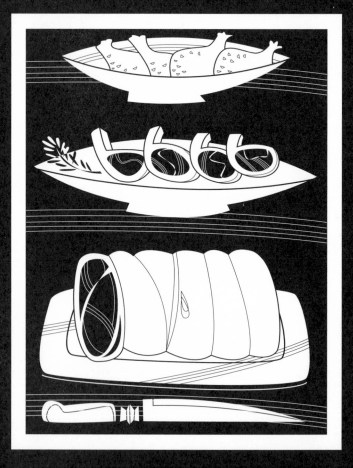

The 20th century proved traumatic for Sussex's native livestock breeds. The Sussex cattle and the Southdown sheep were both once famed across the land for the quality of their meat. But when breeders of both species followed a disastrous policy to miniaturise the size of their stock, both breeds lost commercial headway to larger British and Continental animals. Fortune hasn't been much kinder to the county's poultry keepers as the long tradition of specialist chicken fattening came to an end and was briefly replaced by the intensive broiler house. What large-scale pig farming there had been retreated to the grain-belt counties once more. Game couldn't shake off its rather elitist and difficult image.

It's early days but the 21st century looks a rosier prospect for the consumer seeking out a tastier piece of meat. The growth in the number of farmers' markets, farm shops and box schemes selling high-quality meat direct from farm to the public has meant that it is now a great deal easier to find good, often breed-specific, locally reared meat and poultry. Well-prepared game, too, is easier to source with a series of game dealers spread right across the county, and there now seems to be a growing determination to bring this potentially most free-range of meats to a wider public.

LAMB

SOUTHDOWN RETURNS

Sussex supports one sheep breed entirely native to the county – the Southdown – and shares another with its eastern neighbour Kent, the Romney, formerly the Romney Marsh. Both breeds have been highly developed and improved, evolving over many years to meet the demands of their differing terrains, and also their markets.

The Southdown breed has been in existence since medieval times but it was during the 18th century that gentleman farmers like John Ellman of Glynde made such extraordinary improvements to the breed and marketed it so effectively that the expansion of the Southdowns across the country to both east and west was unparalleled. The Reverend Arthur Young, in his *General View of the Agriculture of the County of Sussex*, wrote in awe that 'the whole tract of the Downs in their full extent, is stocked with sheep, and the amazing numbers they keep is one of the most singular circumstances in the husbandry of England.'

Maximum production of both sheep and wheat was the aim of the 19th-century Downland farmers and the two forms of farming were entirely interlinked – in complete contrast to sheep and arable farming today. During daylight hours the sheep grazed on the upper slopes of the Downs, sometimes eating specifically-sown crops – perhaps turnips, cabbage or potatoes. In the evening, the sheep were brought down to small enclosures – folds – on the lower slopes. These more fertile areas of the Downs would be later sown to arable crops like wheat and barley and needed concentrated doses of good fertiliser which the sheep, penned in for the night, would amply provide. In the morning the sheep would be turned back out on the hill, perhaps taken to the very steepest land first of all to nibble hungrily on any encroaching scrub.

Wheat and sheep were thus inextricably linked in this highly labour-intensive – and therefore expensive – form of farming. The gentlemen farmers of the Southdowns – many of them, like Ellman, tenants to large estates – were characterised by their uniform of black frock coat and tall top hats. Even today, Wealden farmers still mutter about 'millionaires' row', referring to the grassy hillsides that once supported this highly profitable sheep and corn farming system.

The great agricultural depression of the late 19th century started the decline of the Southdown sheep, at first slowly enough. As the new railroads across America linked the grain belt of the Mid-West with the eastern seaboard ports, grain started to flood into Britain and the price of wheat tumbled. The cost of shipping wheat between New York and Liverpool fell by half between 1830 and 1880, and by half again from 1880 to 1914. And as the grain price tumbled, the area of land under arable cultivation fell and the sheep numbers accordingly fell too. Prices improved for farmers during World War I, but labour was now at a premium – many of their shepherds were called up to serve, swapping downland hollows and barrows for the trenches of the Somme. But as late as the 1920s the sheep still poured off the neighbouring hills into towns and villages like Lewes and Findon for the annual sheep fairs, choking the lanes and roads for hours at a time. And there was still outrage in the late 1920s when one farmer brought a group of Welsh-bred Kerry fat lambs into Lewes market – they were penned off well away from all of the other sheep as if in quarantine for some dread disease.

A deliberate and disastrous breeding policy to 'miniaturise' the Southdown breed in the mid-20th century resulted in Southdown rams too small to mate successfully with any other mainstream breed of ewe, and the numbers of Southdown, now pygmy in economic terms too, plummeted, until in 1987 they were declared a 'rare breed'.

And now? Twenty years on, the Southdown is once more on the road to mainstream status. This is largely due to the stubborn determination of Southdown breeders once more to improve the stock by adding size and improving conformation of the animals through selective breeding, even at one point shipping in rams descended from pre-miniaturised flocks from New Zealand. Interestingly, one of the leading players in this breed revival and 're-improvement' was John Craig, a farmer at

Gote Farm, Glyndebourne – farming barely a mile or two away from the farm of the mighty Southdown improver, Ellman.

Another factor in the breed's popularity is perhaps a greater public awareness amongst consumers that the only way to keep a breed alive is to eat it. A scheme to promote the progeny of Southdown rams has been up and running for three years now, making Southdown meat available across the county at selected butchers and farm shops, and there are farms across the region producing lamb for direct sale at farmers' markets. Meat from a Southdown lamb is undeniably a little fattier than from some of the more popular sheep breeds like the Texel, for example, but Southdown meat is very sweet and is said to pick up its taste from the wide diversity of grasses and wild herbs that grow on the Downs. Eastbourne organic farmer Richard Brown, who since 2003 has run a butcher's shop just outside the town at Willingdon, is careful to send his Southdown sheep for slaughter when they're still relatively small and before they get too fat. For this reason, he says, Southdown mutton is still a bit of a rarity.

The Southdown has historically often been crossed with its close neighbour, the Romney. One of the oldest sheep breeds in the country, the Romney is a big tough handsome sheep, admirably adapted to its natural habitat, the Romney Marshes on the Sussex-Kent border. Romney sheep farmers like Martin Hole, who farms on the Pevensey marshes, compare its meat favourably to the Southdown; though well-marbled, the meat is less fatty, he says. Prized in particular for their wool, the sheep are renowned for their ability to get a good living off grass alone, in complete contrast therefore to the Southdown. A feature of the Romney Marshes is the high numbers of sheep to the acre that the area can sustain – a tribute, Hole says, both to the quality of the grazing land and also to the grazing animal. The breed is supposed to have adapted to its damp native terrain in being particularly resistant to foot-rot and liver fluke. While the Romney forms the backbone of the New Zealand lamb flock, numbers of Romneys have fallen in England over the years as more prolific cross-bred sheep like the North of England Mule have become more popular.

IDEAS FOR SHOULDERS & BREASTS OF LAMB

Most butchers say that while legs and racks of lamb fly out of their shops, shoulders and breasts are a little harder to sell. Although fattier than the leg, this is a plus point; the meat can stand a longer cooking process without drying out.

𝕤 For a summery and fragrant roast, slit the skin of the shoulder with the tip of a sharp knife and insert slivers of garlic and stalks of rosemary and lavender. The lavender adds a delicate perfumed fragrance to the meat.

𝕤 A tasty variation is the *boulangère* method. After an initial half an hour or so of roasting at high temperature, take the garlic-studded shoulder out of the oven and put it to one side. Turn the oven down to about 150°C/gas mark 2. Add a mass of thinly sliced, well-seasoned potato and onion to the tin, moisten with half a litre or so of lamb stock and a little wine and place the shoulder on top. Continue roasting for about three hours or until the lamb is very tender. Take the lamb out of the tin, and leave covered in foil in a warm place. Turn the oven up to a high heat. Gently stir the vegetables and when the oven is hot return the tin to crisp the potatoes.

𝕤 Boned out by the butcher, the whole shoulder can be stuffed (garlic, breadcrumbs, herbs) and slow-roasted. Cut into cubes, boned shoulder makes excellent meat for stewing (tagines, curries, casseroles) as the long slow cooking makes the meat meltingly tender.

𝕤 The breast of a lamb is a long, thin piece of meat well-supplied with rib bones. It can be boned out by your butcher and makes a tasty slow-roasting joint rolled up around a lemon, herb and breadcrumb stuffing.

𝕤 A traditional French method, breast of lamb *Sainte-Ménehould*, involves simmering the lamb with herbs and vegetables until tender, pulling out the bones, pressing it flat and then coating strips of the cooked meat with mustard, egg and breadcrumbs before grilling it crisp.

𝕤 Breast of lamb can also be used for kebabs over the barbecue. Marinade small cubes of the meat overnight in plenty of lemon, garlic, herbs and even chilli – strong flavours that will cut through the fattiness of the meat.

BEEF

THE HARDY SUSSEX

Unlike the Southdown sheep that was very much a part of Downland farming in Sussex, the 'Sussex' breed of cattle was linked to the very different terrain of the Weald. The Sussex was an animal that had adapted well to tough conditions, capable of not just ekeing out a living but positively flourishing on the challenging terrain that makes up so much of the county. On the more fertile coastal plains of West Sussex between Shoreham and Chichester the Sussex had less hold – in its place were the Devon breeds, milkier cows, bred for a lusher, milder climate. The reputation of the Sussex at the turn of the 19th century was as a fine-quality beef breed, not very milky but producing some of the best meat in the country and worthy of comparison with the other great native English breed, the Hereford.

But the Sussex has had a rocky ride since. While local demand for Sussex beef has always been high, the breed has been so traditionally linked to the most challenging terrain in the entire country that its fate has always been in the hands of some of the most financially insecure farmers in the county. And for many farmers in the area, the beef industry was always a secondary concern in comparison to much of the Weald's traditional reliance on its wheat crop.

With the falling numbers, the national reputation of the Sussex cattle declined and lost ground to the Shorthorns and the Herefords. When the price of wheat fell again after the Napoleonic Wars, many Wealden farmers preferred to re-stock their land with a few dairy cattle instead – milk production was rightly seen as a more reliable way of making money. Sheep numbers on the Downs and the Sussex and Kent marshes were at an all-time high, and the practice of bringing many of these sheep to the Weald for the wet winter months put added pressure on grazing land.

Ironically, in the mid-18th century the salvation of such a Wealden animal lay in the hands of the far wealthier Downland farmers. Farm machinery had now become much lighter and much of the heavy farm labour could now be entrusted to the heavy horse rather than the muscled shoulders of the ox. The Sussex had always been a dual-purpose animal – bred for its draught capability as much as for the quality of its carcass. Now breeders could turn their attention to developing the back end of the animal (where all the prime meat is situated) rather than the front neck and shoulders that had dragged a heavy plough over a claggy clay soil. By the 1880s, the Sussex breed had been improved out of all recognition. It was still the case that most of the breeding of Sussex cattle took place on the Weald – cattle in the area around Mayfield and Bexhill, for example, were much admired – but much of the improving of the breed took place on the southerly Downland slopes.

Improved or not, many of the Wealden herds were dispersed in the late 19th century as more and more farms went over to milk production, and the often unproductive pasture of the Weald was usually unable to support both sorts of cattle.

Like the Southdown sheep, the Sussex breed suffered from the wrong-headed perception, post World War II, that people's eating habits were changing and the small joint of beef was thought to be 'the way forward'. So the Sussex was bred smaller and smaller, while the post-war appetite grew for large amounts of lean beef; this has meant that the vast amount of beef sold nationally over the past 30 years has come from continental-sired animals like the Charolais or Limousin – lean, big-framed animals. Slow to mature, yet quick to run to fat, the short-legged Sussex was seen by many farmers as having limited appeal and largely disappeared from consumer consciousness. However, with growing interest in regional food and the increasing understanding that it's the fat in a joint or a steak that carries the flavour, traditional native breeds like the Sussex are making a comeback. Unsupported at this point by the supermarket network, marketing of the Sussex is left, by and large, to the independent butcher, the farmers' market and by farmers themselves either at markets or directly to local customers.

Andrew Hoad sells his own home-reared Sussex beef at his farm shop at Salehurst, just outside Robertsbridge. Running a mixed farm, the Hoads had originally reared beef cattle from surplus dairy calves brought in from other farms. But as the dairy herds in the area started to disperse, his raw material dried up. He decided to invest in a pedigree herd of Sussex cattle, admiring their calm temperament. And just as his 19th-century ancestors had done before him, he realised that the Sussex simply 'did' much better than other breeds he had farmed – in autumn, when the grass stops growing, the Sussex cattle continued to thrive while his continental cross-cattle dropped condition. His beef is highly sought-after locally – so much so that the shop can barely keep up with demand. Although the Sussex is a stumpy animal in comparison with, say, a Charolais, it has a great depth of carcass. The meat is closely-grained and well-marbled with fat – always a prime consideration for a good steak.

Moreover, enthusiasm for the Sussex breed is starting to be recognised outside the county again. Highfields Farm at Mayfield at present breeds and fattens 200 cattle a year. Its farm manager, former butcher Simon Jenner, now has the chance to raise the kind of animals he was trained to identify as likely to make the best meat. A few years back, Jenner and farm owner Simon Tindall realised that there was no profit in selling cattle through their local livestock market, and that it would be more profitable to target production at specific markets. While selling direct to several butchers in the area, the farm now supplies The Butcher and Grill Restaurant in Battersea, London. Before the restaurant opened, the Sussex beef had to compete in a blind tasting against beef from a continental and a Scottish breed, and the Sussex came out top 'by far'.

It's the local provenance of the beef – valued more than organic status by the retailer – that has proved so essential to the success of the scheme. The cattle graze outside on the farm between April and October, coming into barns when the weather deteriorates to feed on grass silage and maize, barley and peas which Jenner sources from local farms. The cattle only leave the farm for a short 6-mile (10-km) journey to the abattoir at Heathfield, and the carcasses then hang for a minimum of 21 days at the shop. Further retail linkups with London are in the pipeline.

Veal

Finding an economic and worthwhile use for the male calves born to pure dairy cows has always been a problem for dairy farmers, especially when the price of beef is low. The pure Holstein Friesian cows kept by many farmers for their milking parlours make for highly productive dairy animals as the food they consume goes straight to the supply of their enormous and productive udders, rather than padding out their bodies. The male dairy calves that inevitably make up 50 per cent of the cows' progeny have traditionally been laughed out of the beef cattle market because of the lack of muscle on their skinny frames. The solution for many farmers in the past has often been a bullet at birth, or a long journey on a truck to the continent where veal is more popular.

Phil and Stephen Hook at the organic Longleys Farm, in Hailsham, have joined a small but growing band of farmers now raising these calves for beef and 'rose' veal. They sell the slightly larger and better framed animals as beef at two years old, while the true 'coathanger' calves are raised for veal. The two sets of animals are kept in the same way – housed in small groups in straw pens (which they can eat) with plenty of room to move about, and fed concentrates as well as a staggering quantity of milk. A Hook veal calf will drink £500-worth of milk in its six months' lifetime so the resulting product is naturally a little expensive. The result is a highly welfare-friendly rose veal meat certified by the Soil Association, a far cry from the intensively reared white veal meat of the past, with its barred crates and restrictive milk-only diet (both banned in the UK in 1990 and in other EU countries in 2007). The historical concern over veal in Britain is so widespread that reaching out to new customers worried about welfare can be difficult, but veal produced correctly does represent a sensible solution to a problem that is often brushed aside by misplaced sensibility.

PORK

D omesday records show that 150,000 pigs were annually driven into the Wealden woodlands to graze on beech mast and acorns. This practice, known as 'pannage', is thought to have gone back as far as several thousand years BC. The temporary huts or 'dens' that these animal graziers built for themselves went on to form permanent settlements, and the tracks that the animals followed in and out of the woodlands became the roads that we still use today in and out of the High Weald.

But Sussex has never been a prime pork-producing county like, say, Norfolk or Berkshire. It has no 'native' breed of pig like its westerly neighbour, Hampshire, and specialist pork butcheries – still relatively common in the eastern counties – are extremely rare here. Yet pork is very much present in traditional Sussex cooking – bacon and lard are common ingredients in many recipes – and it's certainly the case that until quite recently most country families (and probably many town ones, too) kept the odd pig or two in a sty or outhouse to absorb all the family scraps and waste matter. Large areas of the county are simply unsuitable for widespread pig rearing due to the heaviness of the land – no pig is going to thrive in deep mud.

Over the past 50 years, pigs have been reared indoors on a commercial scale across the country and some of this 'intensive' pig production has taken place in Sussex. But the practice has never been particularly widespread in the county, and high-density indoor pig production has more or less retired to the eastern counties where corn is more plentiful and the piggy infrastructure – grain mills and abattoirs – is still present.

Small-scale pork production flourishes in the county, though, with both abattoirs reporting a regular stream of small producers bringing in one or two pigs each week to supply local butchers and farmers' markets. At Goodwood, 50 saddleback sows roam the 500 acres (200 ha) of estate woodland. The weaned piglets are taken off to be raised in nearby fields but the sows stay in the woods all year round, their powerful noses clearing the scrub as they root in the soil just as their ancestors in Ashdown Forest did thousands of years ago.

At Rushlake Green, David and Erica Turton raise around 170 Landrace pigs a year, with only 30 or so pigs on the farm at any one time. They sell their fresh pork, bacon and sausages at farmers' markets around East Sussex. The advantage of the pig, as David Turton points out, is that it is very easy to add value to it, and after a career raising pigs in the county, he is happy now to be 'niche marketing' a small amount of pork to a specific clientele rather than trying to raise large quantities of cheap pork. High-quality bacon and sausages sell themselves all year round, he says, and 'across the social divide'.

Turton buys in newly weaned pigs from a county council farm in Essex and takes them on to pork and bacon weight. Pigs for fresh pork are traditionally killed earlier so that the meat is more tender and pigs for bacon are killed later for maximum size. Most British pig producers have adopted the continental system of raising all their pigs to bacon weight and this has resulted in a lot of tough pork. Perhaps the trouble is that we haven't also adopted the continental expertise with pork that results in those temples to pig processing, the French charcuteries.

Local abattoirs

For many producers, their proximity to a slaughterhouse is a unique selling-point for their product. Tottingworth slaughterhouse to the east of Heathfield has 1000 clients on its lists – varying from people bringing in one or two animals once a year to the larger wholesalers bringing in lorry-loads every week. Sarah Wareham inherited the business first established by her grandfather Dennis Browning in the 1960s. Her business has changed out of all recognition over the past 10 years – between a quarter to half of all animals killed now are from small producers either selling meat at farmers' markets and farm shops or for home consumption. The business opened its own cutting room in 2005 to butcher animals to customers' specifications, and has trebled its output since.

POULTRY & EGGS

HIGGLING & CRAMMING

While nowadays we associate the forced feeding of poultry with the duck and goose farming of south-western France, we've largely (or maybe conveniently) forgotten that only 75 years ago a highly developed, if extremely localised, form of forced poultry feeding was flourishing in the heart of Sussex.

In West Sussex, the area around Northchapel, north of Petworth was described in 1801 as being 'famous for fowls'. The East Sussex tradition started in a small enough way with 'higglers' – itinerant chicken carriers – buying young chickens from farms around the area and either fattening the birds themselves or selling them on to other small farms for fattening. Artificial fattening, or 'cramming' as it was known, is first mentioned in the Heathfield area in the mid-1830s. Farmers bought three- to four-month-old birds from the higglers and kept them on a diet of oats for another three to four months until the birds were ready to cram by tubing a mixture of oats, skimmed milk and fat straight down their throats twice a day. The cramming lasted a fortnight or three weeks, after which the birds were killed.

What started as a small-scale concern rapidly changed into what, at times during the century, became the most profitable agricultural practice of the area. Poultry rearing, like dairymaiding, had traditionally been the preserve of women (tending chickens being relatively light work), providing eggs for cooking, birds for the table and a little extra pocket-money on the side. By mid-century, chicken-cramming had become a highly-organised local industry. The extraordinary expansion of the railway network mid-century meant that poultry could be quickly transported to the valuable London markets. Here poultry was in great demand – the fashion for French-style cooking saw the move away from the roast beef of old English fare towards the chicken quenelles and the capon chaudfroid of French cuisine.

Some farmers were feeding just a few birds in this way each week, but there were others cramming chicken on a much bigger scale. This was early 'intensive' chicken production long before the emergence of the broiler house. Birds would be housed in sheds, long coops divided into pens, five or six birds to each pen. By the end of the century well over 1000 tonnes (900 tons) of chicken was leaving Heathfield and Uckfield every year.

The chicken industry lost headway during World War I, when foreign imports of grain dried up and the cost of domestic grain rose sharply. Although the 1930s brought further farming depression and chicken cramming became profitable once more, it was the beginning of the end of the Heathfield trade. Roads were becoming more important than rails for transportation, and higglers were no longer needed, as the farmer fatteners could deal directly with the chicken producers. When poultry production was sidelined during World War II as being non-essential, flock numbers dwindled. And with the introduction of the new broiler-style houses that could be built anywhere and tended to by anyone, chicken farming became a truly modern factory industry, rather than a peasant trade to be taken up and put away as demand rose or dwindled. But perhaps it's significant that it was at the edge of this historically important cramming region that the first true factory chicken farm was established at Buxted in the mid-1950s. Within 10 years, the company was producing 500,000 birds a week.

Since then, large-scale indoor chicken production has mostly gone from the county, retreating back to the grain heartlands of the country, leaving in its wake a small number of farmers raising high-quality birds.

At the weekly Wednesday morning market at East Dean, Michael Vine sells the chicken he has raised at his poultry farm on the outskirts of Hailsham. The farm lies just a few yards up the road from where his great grandmother was rearing poultry at the end of the 19th century. An ancient photograph on Vine's stall shows a rather grim-faced woman amongst a family group, a goose ready for plucking lying prone on her lap. Vine, by contrast, is much more cheerful – perhaps because these days the plucking process is somewhat more mechanised – but with the farm killing just over 250 birds a week, production is still small enough for each bird to come under his eagle eye. The majority of his trade is to local shops and restaurants but a sizeable proportion is to retail customers at farmers' markets in the area, or to locals who want to come to the farm to pick up a chicken or two. The chickens are reared indoors, but the birds grow more slowly than under an intensive broiler-house system, so they have time to develop flavour and have plenty of room to wander around, scratch and peck. Buyers are welcome to have a look around the farm to see for themselves the quality of the husbandry. The birds are killed on the farm – quickly and expertly. Vine also raises around 300 Kelly turkeys for the Christmas market, some white, some bronze.

Further west, Glyn Thomas raises 1400 or so free-range turkeys for the Christmas market at Holmansbridge Farm just north of Cooksbridge. The Holmansbridge turkeys are still plucked by hand – Thomas just feels that the birds look better for being hand plucked – but fortunately for the family's sanity they're joined in the task each year by a keen group of local volunteers wanting to get into the Christmas spirit, sitting in a circle singing along to carols. Nothing has changed really for a hundred years, Thomas says, except now everyone has to wear masks.

The Thomases are also well known for their free-range eggs – at just 5800 birds it's a small unit (by modern standards) but they supply some high-profile clients like the well-regarded vegetarian restaurant Terre à Terre in Brighton and the Jolly Sportsman gastro-pub down the road at East Chiltington. The laying hens spread over the fields behind the house are a mix of Columbian Blacktails and Bovan Goldlines – 'nice, relatively calm' birds that even seem to cope reasonably well with the odd hot-air balloon ascent nearby. Perhaps they're lulled by their daily dose of Southern FM (although they listen to classical music, if Mr Thomas's mother, Ann, is doing the rounds that morning).

As a bonus, Mrs Thomas started to make meringues to sell at Lewes Farmers' Market because she thought the stall looked rather dull just piled high with egg boxes. She now supplies meringues for local caterers who don't have the time to make them themselves (meringues consume rather a lot of valuable oven time).

GAME

BIRDS, BEASTS & RABBITS

G ame – venison aside – had been available to all until an Act of Parliament in 1671 was passed that prohibited the killing of game for the majority of the population. From this point on, only 'qualified persons' (that is, wealthy landowners), were allowed to kill game, and masked poaching became a capital offence from 1723 under the notorious Black Act.

Sussex has its fair share of large estates, many of which lie in a string along the South Downs – from Cowdray in the west of the county to Glynde and Firle in the east. Downland estates of this nature have long been considered prime shooting territory because experienced sportsmen prefer the challenge of shooting birds rising up over the hills; birds on the flatter ground of much of the Weald, say, don't tend to fly up in the air in the same way. David and Sherry Douglas sell a wide variety of game at their farm, South Brockwells Farm, just to the west of Uckfield. They source around 20 different kinds of game from Sussex farms and estates like those at Glynde, Pangdean and Framfield. Between October and January, Douglas collects the game from each estate in its feathered state and takes it for processing to game specialists V. J. Game at Broad Oak each Thursday ready for the farm shop's weekend opening. A wide range of game is sold including partridge, pheasant – what he calls 'beginner's game' – pigeon and venison, which he says is slowly becoming more popular. Douglas is encouraged by the interest shown by younger people in eating game and proffers much-needed cooking advice for game 'virgins'.

Rabbits were introduced to Britain by the Normans and for centuries were kept in warrens as a supply for meat and fur – coney farming was particularly practised in the Ashdown Forest where remains of 'pillow mounds'– man-made rabbit warrens–can still be seen. Imports during the 19th century from Holland and Belgium and, later, from Australia, started to make rabbit farming uneconomic. The 1880 Act that finally gave tenant farmers the right to shoot vermin on the land they farmed further undermined the finances of the organised warrener and the domestic farmed rabbit all but disappeared.

Wild rabbits have flourished again in recent years, presenting a serious pest to both farmers and other landowners. Seven rabbits will eat as much as one sheep, so grassland becomes unproductive for sheep or cattle grazing if rabbit numbers go unchecked. The damage to expensive arable crops is even more costly – a burrow of hungry rabbits can cost a farmer thousands of pounds in lost wheat or barley.

Andy Weller is typical of many shooters. By prior arrangement with local landowners, he shoots around 2500 rabbits a year, keeping the rabbit population down to manageable levels . The healthiest Sussex rabbits, he says, are those that live on the Downs because their burrows in the free-draining chalky ground are dry even in the wettest winters. Rabbits that he shoots on the heavy clay ground of the Weald are leaner and lack the fat reserves around the kidneys that are the sure sign of a prime rabbit for the pot. His hunting career started at the age of six, ferreting on the hills around Selmeston during World War II when rabbit meat was an important supplement to the meagre meat ration of the time. Nowadays he prefers to shoot his rabbits rather than ferret them – ferreting is a highly time-consuming affair as it means netting each viable rabbit hole in a burrow. Weller shoots at night from a four-by-four vehicle with a rifle rather than a shotgun so as to leave the rabbit free of the 'shot' that is apt to be a culinary hazard of the wild rabbit. The ideal cooking age for a wild rabbit is around nine months to a year, when it's old enough to be flavoursome but still young enough to be tender. Detecting a rabbit's age can be a difficult affair for the layman. Tearing the ear of a (dead) rabbit is apparently one sure sign, as is cracking its jaw. Ease of skinning is also a good sign. But for those of us who buy our rabbits skinned and decapitated we're more likely to have to rely simply on the recommendation of a good butcher or game dealer. All good butchers in the region should be able to supply a source of fine, local rabbit.

Venison Stew

A rich, boozy stew that's simple to make. Start it a day or two before you want to serve it as it benefits from a night in the fridge.

INGREDIENTS
SERVES 4

• *Streaky bacon, 250 g*
• *Diced venison, 1 kg*
• *Shallots, 250 g*
• *A sprig of thyme, 3 bay leaves, 3 cloves of garlic*
• *Zest and juice of an orange*
• *A bottle of robust red wine*
• *Port, 250 ml*
• *A double brandy*
• *Button mushrooms, 250 g*

INSTRUCTIONS

1. Dice the bacon and fry it in a large-lidded, heavy-based cooking pan until the fat runs. Lift out the bacon with a slotted spoon and set to one side on a plate. Pat the venison with a kitchen towel if it looks a little wet and fry it in batches until browned, setting each batch aside on the plate with the bacon. Add a little oil to the pan as you go if you need some.

2. Pour the red wine and the port into a separate saucepan and bring it slowly to a simmer.

3. Turn the heat down in the main pan a little and fry the shallots for about five minutes, stirring well. Add the herbs and the garlic and fry for another minute or so. Return the meat to the pan, pour in the brandy and flame it. Pour in the wine and add the zest and juice of the orange. Bring the pan to a gentle simmer, put on the lid, and let the venison bubble away very gently for an hour to an hour and a half, stirring occasionally. Then take the pan off the heat, let the stew cool and put it in the fridge overnight.

4. A couple of hours before you want to eat, take the stew from the fridge, skim off any fat and set the pan on the hob to heat up gently. Bring the stew to a simmering point and let it cook on for an hour. Fry the button mushrooms quickly in a little butter and oil and add them to the pan to cook for a further 30 to 45 minutes. Test to see that the meat is tender and serve, perhaps with some very creamy mashed potatoes and buttered cabbage.

Either cook the stew in two one-and-a-half-hour sessions, or cook it completely one day and merely heat it up on the hob or in the oven the next day until piping hot.

PART THREE

DAIRY

Historically Sussex has never been one of the 'milky' counties like Somerset or Gloucestershire, long-famed for the quality of their cheesemaking or the particular superiority of their butter. The native breed of cattle, the Sussex, was always a working and fattening animal, the dairy aspect of the beast a secondary concern. Until the last third of the 19th century, Sussex dairymaking seems to have been on an entirely small-scale basis, supplying domestic needs and local markets. Until the mid-19th century and the building of the railways – the first section of the London to Brighton railway between Haywards Heath and Norwood was completed in 1841 – city or town farms supplied most urban areas, it being difficult to transport fresh milk any distance due to the lack of refrigeration and the long journey times.

MILK

AGAINST THE GRAIN

The overall climate of the county is historically against extensive dairy production. Sussex is a dry county in comparison to the mild and damp climate of, say, the south-west. Downland farmers were traditionally inhibited from largescale dairy farming by a lack of water – both in terms of actual drinking water for stock, and in terms of lush pasture for both summer grazing and for taking hay crops for winter feeding. By the turn of the 19th century, Sussex Downland farms were mostly given over to sheep and corn production – which for much of the century was highly profitable.

On the Weald, the corn harvest was also seen by tenant farmers as the crop that paid the landlord his rent. But here arable production was riskier owing to the heavy nature of much of the land. During the Napoleonic Wars, when the price of grain was attractively high for farmers, any Wealden land that could be cultivated had been put to the plough. Yet even when the price of wheat tumbled again after the war ended and imports could once more enter the country, the Sussex farmers of the Weald still continued to grow corn wherever possible – probably because many of these farms couldn't actually afford to change their farming practices. The dry summer conditions meant that establishing permanent pasture for cows to graze might take years and the often cash-strapped Wealden farmers couldn't wait that long to take a living from the land.

With the opening of the London-to-Brighton railway and the subsequent network of lines that was quickly established, Sussex now seemed very much closer to London. Before this, every journey northwards had meant a coach trek through what was often a quagmire of a Wealden landscape. For the first time, major towns and cities like London could get their milk from the countryside rather than rely on frequently far-from-satisfactory city farms for supply. A farm's proximity to the railway (and therefore to urban markets) became more important than the traditional qualities of soil type and climate. The numbers of cows in milk in Sussex increased 70 per cent between 1870 and 1911.

Liquid milk sales increased dramatically during the latter half of the 19th century and farmers from the south-west saw opportunities for more profitable milk production in the populous south-east – the population of Sussex as a whole had gone from around 160,000 in 1801 to 550,000 in 1891. At the turn of the century there was an overwhelming influx of farmers into the county from traditional dairying counties like Somerset and Devon, bringing with them extensive dairy expertise.

As the grain prices tumbled in the years before World War I, many of the traditional downland farms gradually became unprofitable. It became quite usual for a Downland tenant farmer to give up his farm to a 'shire-man' from the West Country. Cows milked in the West Country in the morning could even be loaded up onto trains, and transported to their new home in Sussex in time for evening milking.

The can-do attitude of the new breed of dairy farmer was completely different to that of the highly conservative corn growers of the past who rather felt that dairy farming was beneath them. Harry Carr of Kingston remembered seeing one of his well-to-do Downland farming neigh-bours going off to Lewes in his polished carriage drawn by its team of matching grey horses, wearing his black frock coat with his tall black top hat – the uniform of the Downland gentleman farmer. He'd been hunting to hounds on the previous Saturday just as he had hunted twice a week throughout the season. Carr later found out that the farmer was going into town to file for bankruptcy – but appearances were maintained to the last.

It was only milk production that ensured the survival of many once highly profitable Sussex arable/sheep farms during the 1930s when grain prices fell further. On some of the most productive land in the county only small acreages of land were sown to wheat, which was then grown not for its seedhead, but for its straw as essential bedding for the only prof-itable thing on the farm – the dairy herd.

Post-war, dairy farming entered a brief golden age of profitability. Jim Harrison at Rudgwick in West Sussex was milking 20 cows in the early 1950s and in less than 20 years had expanded to milking over a thousand cows. Until milk quotas were introduced in 1984 farm profits could be ploughed back into buying more cows and updating a farm's infrastructure. After 1984, the purchase of quota absorbed much of the profit a farmer was making.

With the de-regulation of the Milk Marketing Board, the milk price dropped dramatically and has never really stabilised. The number of herds and the number of cows being milked in the county has dropped sharply over the past 20 years. The generally low milk price is probably the greatest problem for most farmers, but there is also a serious shortage of skilled labour willing to take on twice-daily milking starting at 4 am. These are national issues, of course, but, bearing in mind that Sussex dairying has always been at a distinct disadvantage in terms of climate in comparison to the western side of the country, any downturn bites very hard here. And as many dairy farms have disappeared, the pressure on the remaining ones is all the greater as the infrastructure based around the local industry – the suppliers, the machinery specialists, and the pool of expertise – starts to wane. Add to this the very high land and property prices of the region, and it's easy to see why many farmers often choose retirement or diversification over continued investment in what can be a very marginal operation.

But it's not all doom and gloom. At the time of writing, the milk price has improved from 17p to 25p in the past 12 months and some dairy farms have chosen to add value to their milk product. Some have turned to direct retailing – either supplying their own farm shops, or undertaking milk deliveries both retail and wholesale. Some are converting to organic production to benefit from the slightly higher prices – others have turned to making ice-cream, perhaps, or creating links with other businesses, perhaps supplying milk to cheesemakers.

The Goodwood Estate to the east of Chichester runs its own 3000-acre organic farm which is almost entirely self-sufficient. All the food crops for the stock – wheat, barley, oats, clover and lupins, for example, are grown on the farm. An integral part of the farm is the estate's 200, mostly Shorthorn, dairy cows. The cows arrived with manager Karl Barton in 2001 from Dorset (a 21st-century example of another West Country dairy specialist coming into the county) but the Shorthorn had traditionally been one of the dairy cows of choice in the region before the Holstein Friesian started to dominate the industry in the early 20th century. The cows are crossed either to pure Shorthorn bulls for dairy replacement, or to Sussex bulls for beef. The Shorthorn, historically more of a dual-purpose breed (both milk and meat), has a heavier frame than the Holstein and so the pure Shorthorn males are still highly suitable for beef production. A flexible milk contract with a milk wholesale company has allowed the farm to start processing about half of its own milk by converting a shed on the farm to a spotless new pasteurising, separating and bottling dairy. With its racetrack, motor circuit, hotel and restaurants, the estate naturally has its own ready-made market on site (the estate absorbs about 60 per cent of the entire estate farm production), but the farm also supplies its own farm shop as well as local shops in the area.

One perhaps surprising new trend in the county is the growing number of farms selling raw (unpasteurised) milk. No less than three farms now supply raw milk in just one small area of East Sussex between Lewes and Hailsham. Middle Farm at Firle sells raw Jersey milk from its farm shop, as well as supplying milk to local cheesemakers; two others, Gote Farm at Ringmer, which sells at Lewes Farmers' Market, and a third, Longleys Farm, near Hailsham, have even established their own milk rounds in the immediate areas to their farms. Phil Hook and son Stephen deliver around 1000 bottles of milk each week – just a tenth of their production but already 25 per cent of their income. Bottles at Longleys are washed in the family dishwasher – 51 at a time. By law, raw milk retailers have to carry health warnings on the labelling of their milk that it 'may contain organisms harmful to human health'. However, the retailers themselves extol the health benefits of raw milk, claiming the possibility that raw milk, amongst other things, may decrease the chances of children suffering allergy-related diseases.

The bio-dynamic dairy herd

At Sharpethorne, the bio-dynamic Plaw Hatch Farm runs its own raw milk delivery service to locals in the Forest Row area. It's a 'really inefficient' service according to Tom Ventham, who manages the farming side of the co-operative, as the van is often taking just one pint up to a house at the end of a very long lane. But über-efficiency is not really the point of Plaw Hatch, who very much see their farm as a service to the local community as well as an entirely self-sustaining operation to the 25 or so people on the payroll. The farm runs 45 horned red and white Meuse Rhine Issel cows – a Dutch dual-purpose breed which makes for a meaty sort of dairy cow with perhaps a third of the milk production capability of the white and black Holstein.

The bio-dynamic movement that is central to everything that goes on at Plaw Hatch, is based on the research and teachings of Rudolf Steiner who, in the early 20th century, argued that a strong spiritual element was vital to good farming practice. The horned aspect of the dairy cow is absolutely central to this bio-dynamic ethos as the horns are seen as vital to the life-force of the cow. Removing a cow's horns (which contain a highly developed nervous system), the movement maintains, allows these vital forces within the animal to dissipate; cows with intact horns, by contrast, are said to be able to re-absorb these vital forces, which are then eventually expelled from the cow in the form of highly fertile manure. By drinking the milk of a horned animal, the theory goes, we are taking in milk containing more natural vitality because it comes from an animal with more life-force. The milk is unpasteurised because pasteurising it would take 'substance' out of the milk.

According to Ventham, Plaw Hatch's customers are very sensitive to how the character of the milk varies according to the time of year and even to the particular area of pasture that the cows are grazing. A rather wet and reedy area of the farm might mean that the milk tastes a little sharp and if customers ring up concerned about this, Ventham seems merely pleased that they've noticed. Next week, after all, the cows will be in a different field, and the milk will taste a little sweeter again.

Ventham claims that the lack of the dairy smell that tends to hang around the average dairy farm is absent from Plaw Hatch because the animals aren't fed the high-protein diet that most dairy cows consume; the Plaw Hatch cows graze grass in the summer, and munch on only conserved grass (hay) for the six months of the year that they spend indoors. A third of the milk produced by the farm goes straight into glass bottles for sale, a third is turned into yogurt and cream, and a third is

RICE PUDDING

A stove-top rice pudding made like a risotto. You could add a few drops of rosewater to the cooked pudding, or, for a vanilla flavour, drop in a vanilla pod when you add the first measure of milk.

INGREDIENTS
SERVES 4

- *Knob of butter*
- *Pudding or Arborio rice, 200 g*
- *Water, 200 ml*
- *Salt, ½ teaspoon*
- *Milk, approximately 800 ml*
- *Caster sugar, 2 heaped tablespoons*
- *Cinnamon, for dusting*

INSTRUCTIONS

1. Melt the butter in a heavy-based saucepan over low heat and, before it bubbles, add the rice (no need to wash). Stir it in gently so that the rice is coated with the butter and then add the water and salt. Turn the heat up a little and as soon as the rice has absorbed the water add about a third of the milk and sugar.

2. Let the rice just simmer away very gently, and when the milk has been absorbed add half the remaining milk, stirring from time to time to ensure that the rice doesn't stick to the bottom of the pan. Finally add the last of the milk and when this has been absorbed check for sweetness and tenderness – the pudding should be soft and creamy.

3. Serve dusted with cinnamon.

turned into cheese by Sue who runs the dairy side of the farm. Yogurts are flavoured with whatever happens to be in season in the 15 acres of garden and 12 poly-tunnels. A basket of raspberries is brought in from the garden, and within a minute the fruit is being picked over and washed ready for inclusion in today's batch.

The most popular cheese that the farm produces is its cheddar, Plaw Hatch, made using animal rennet, in contrast to most of the cheeses in the county, not for any spiritual reason but because it 'makes a better cheddar'. The previous cheese-maker at Plaw Hatch used to make a semi-soft cheese, Dewpond, but Sue makes feta because 'she likes it'. It is a striking reminder that on a farm like this the well-being and fulfilment of its community of workers is just as important as that of its stock.

CHEESE

A GROWING SUCCESS

The past 10 to 15 years have seen an extraordinary blossoming of the Sussex cheese industry. Dedicated cheese shops like Say Cheese in Lewes routinely stock around 30 or so different local county cheeses and the numbers are growing all the time, from soft white ewes' milk cheeses like Flower Marie to a bio-dynamic raw cows'-milk cheddar such as Plaw Hatch Mature. South African-born cheese-maker Eddie Bestbier and his wife Deborah have recently entered the Sussex scene after a career cheesemaking in Holland and setting up cheese factories in Australia and Canada. Their repertoire – including a very popular Sussex blue and a range of different Dutch Boerekaas cheeses, some spiced – adds another 16 or so cheeses to the Sussex cheeseboard. They have taken a 'massive gamble' Deborah Bestbier says, selling up their business and home in Australia to come to Britain to be near her family. Their business runs from a converted barn just south of Five Ashes, near Mayfield, and opens during the week for tastings.

One of the longest established Sussex cheesemakers is Rob Bookham, the son of a Surrey accountant. Following a three-year course in agriculture at Plumpton Agricultural College, he went to work for an Italian family who had bought an English sporting estate close to Gatwick. Large cheese producers in Italy, the Italians were keen to capitalise on the high butterfat content of English milk to make a parmesan-style cheese using vegetable rennet that Italian vegetarians could eat. Amongst other strict criteria, Italian parmesan must be made with animal rennet to comply with strict Parmigiano Reggiano standards.

Specialised cheese equipment, including the vast cone-shaped copper vats were brought over from Italy and production began in 1985. Initially Bookham was making cheese in England that was then shipped back to Italy to be matured in the cheese banks of the Parma region. At the height of production he was making three tonnes of cheese a day, seven days a week but, as the price of the pound rose and the lira fell eight years ago, it was no longer economically viable to make the cheese for export back to Italy, so Bookham decided to buy the cheese back and start selling it here in England. So little artisan cheese was being made in the south of England at the time that he was asked to sell the Twineham Grange cheese at the newly established Winchester farmers' markets as there was no cheese producer in Hampshire at the time.

Officially known as Twineham Grange but also as 'Farmer's Hand' (try saying it aloud), a third of production is now sold at farmers' markets and food shops locally, a third is bought by British Airways for their in-flight meals (used as a garnish in a sundried tomato salad) and a third is sold through Sainsbury's and Budgen's supermarkets nationwide. Bookham now has his own storage facilities and specialist packing equipment in West Sussex so that he no longer needs to send his cheese to Italy for maturing – essential, he feels, to lower the cheese's 'carbon footprint'. The whey by-product left over after the curd has been cooked and formed is used for making ricotta cheese. The Bookhams use this in turn to make a range of fillings for their own ravioli. In addition, they make a tonne of wrapped butter pats or, as Bookham calls them, 'gold bars' each week.

Bookham now sources his entire milk supply from a farm outside Horsham on the Sussex-Surrey border. The two businesses have gone into partnership to produce a new cheese, Sussex Charmer – a cross between Cheddar and Parmesan – even investing in their own milk tanker to transport the milk from farm to dairy. The cheesemaking process can thus be started at the farm, rather than at the dairy, and the milk kept at the right temperature on its short journey to the dairy, rather than refrigerating the milk and having to bring it back up to temperature on arrival at Twineham.

Just over 10 miles to the east of Twineham, the other side of Haywards Heath, Mark Hardy makes both sheep's and cows' milk cheese at his business, High Weald Dairy, at Horsted Keynes. It was while he was attending Cirencester Agricultural College that Hardy became conscious of the advantage of milking sheep as opposed to cows – not only was there a low capital outlay, but there was none of the bureaucracy of the quota system that complicates the bovine milking parlour.

A proposed linkup with a Turkish Cypriot identified a real market for the sheep's milk that Hardy was starting to produce – halloumi, the salty, fibrous cheese synonymous with Cypriot cuisine. The cheese is made in a different manner to traditional British cheeses – no starter culture is needed and, after the curd has been drained of the whey, the curd is cooked at high temperature, which gives the cheese its unique texture. The cheese is then brine-cured, like feta, which gives it a long shelf life. Halloumi is unusual in that it is almost always eaten cooked – either fried or grilled; a vegetarian 'bacon', as Hardy says.

At the time, no-one was officially importing the cheese into the country so the significant Cypriot population in the Green Lanes area of North London was reliant on community members bringing the cheese back with them after visits to the island. When the proposal with his contact fell through for lack of a cheesemaker, Hardy, faced with an ever-growing store of frozen milk and no market, set off for Cyprus to learn how to make the cheese himself.

Production started in 1987 at the family farm at Duddleswell in a small barn hastily converted to a dairy. Hardy also started making a hard ewes' milk cheese – Duddleswell – a cross between Cheddar and Wensleydale, as well as a light, soft cheese called Sussex Slipcote. A traditional English cheese, the term 'slip cote' may refer to its origins as 'a little piece, or slip, of cottage cheese' or, more entertainingly, it could refer to the habit that the cheese had of bursting out of its skin during the maturing process.

Most of the milking sheep in Britain are Frieslands, the 'Holstein Friesian' of the sheep world. Routinely producing three or four lambs at lambing (most breeds just produce one or two), the Friesland is thus an intensely milky sheep and is famed for its docility. The main trouble, Hardy admits, is not rounding up the sheep for milking – they tear towards the dairyman at the first rattle of a bucket – it's getting them to leave the building again once they've been milked.

Hardy stopped milking his own sheep in 1992 when he realised that he didn't have enough land to produce the quantities of milk he had started to need, so he now sources his milk from selected sheep farmers in the south of England. In 2003, the dairy moved to a converted grain store in a farm in Horsted Keynes, whose cows (literally a stone's throw from the dairy) now provide milk for the range of cows' milk cheeses he makes alongside the sheep's milk ones. The harder cheeses, like the Tremain's Organic Cheddar, are made in the summer when there's a glut of milk from the animals out at pasture.

So the county can now offer a really diverse selection of local cheeses to customers: hard or soft; goat, cow or sheep; traditional English or traditional Mediterranean; even Dutch-style. It's an astonishing record for a county with comparatively little milk and even less of a cheese-making tradition.

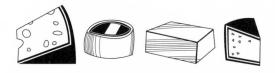

PART FOUR

FRUIT & VEGETABLES

Until relatively recently, most Sussex dwellings, both urban and rural, would have boasted an orchard and kitchen garden (or nearby allotment). Knowledge of how to grow fruit and vegetables and how to process the crop into preserves to last through the year would have been common to almost all – from the grand country squire to his lowliest itinerant worker. So, while commercial production of fruit and vegetables for export from the county has waxed and waned over time, there has always been, and remains, a rich tradition of fruit and vegetable growing here.

The commercial production that exists in Sussex today is governed primarily by soil type and local micro-climates and few counties in England can claim such a variety. From the coastal alluvial soils of the Chichester Plain with its high, light intensity to the sheltered patches of greensand nestling between the Weald and the north escarpment of the South Downs, these variable environments invite an intricate and complex pattern of cropping.

FRUIT

A VARIED CROP

As a fruit-growing county, Sussex has rather been overshadowed by its neighbour, Kent. Much of the terrain – the dry, chalky subsoil of the Downs and the heavy clay land of the Weald – is unsuitable for many sorts of large-scale fruit farming, but where soil type is helpful, the county's soft climate and proximity to London have at times brought fine opportunities to fruit growers.

By the mid-19th century, Sussex fruit growers were benefiting from the growth in rail transport that could for the first time whisk delicate and high-quality fruit quickly around the country, but most particularly to London and of course the very rapidly expanding Sussex towns. Between the 1860s and the 1950s, Worthing, owing to the high quality of its soil, climate and light, became famous for its glasshouse market gardening. It's even said that glass from the original Great Exhibition building at Crystal Palace was recycled into at least one market gardener's glasshouse empire in the area.

By 1895 over a thousand tons of high-quality and high-priced fruit were being dispatched mostly to the highly lucrative London markets. Tomatoes, grapes, peaches, melons and strawberries left 'this town of hot houses' on dedicated fruit trains four times a week. Until protective tariffs brought the practice to an end, Worthing even supplied hot-house grapes to France, and figs were grown on some scale in West Tarring. Thought to have originated in the 13th century, these orchards were producing thousands of figs each year by the 19th century and were a well-known tourist attraction. It is even said that a small songbird similar if not identical to the Italian 'Beccafico' or 'figpecker' was seen in the gardens as the figs ripened each year. It came to no other part of England. The county's glasshouses, like the fig orchards, are now mostly gone, many disappearing under housing in the mid- to late 20th century.

Sussex was once famous for its cherries – particularly the village of Ripe where 'Ripe Tarts' were made to celebrate the cherry harvest. Though the original Ripe orchards are now lost, it seems that the fruit is abundant in the county once more. Cars braking to swerve off the road to a cherry caravan parked in a lay-by have become a common sight in the months of June and July over the past five or so years, although it's frustrating that the English cherry season is slightly spoiled by the weeks of highly-travelled not-so-sweet fruit imported from abroad that precedes it. But the recent availability of cherries has been aided by the introduction of dwarfing rootstocks which has meant that the sweet cherry tree has shrunk from the 15- to 20-ft (4.5- to 6-m) giant that it used to be to a much more manageable size. These smaller trees can be netted against birds or even grown under cover to protect them against heavy rain or hail (increasingly a problem as our climate appears to be growing ever more continental). They also bear fruit much earlier than the old giant trees, which remained barren for 10 years and then often became quickly afflicted with bacterial canker.

A seedling for the Victoria plum is said by many sources to have been discovered in Sussex at the village of 'Alderton', which is confusing as Alderton in Sussex doesn't appear to exist on any map. However, Alderton in Suffolk does. Perhaps, the county name is easily confused in abbreviated form. But being the birthplace of England's most famous plum is no cause for great celebration anyway. Jane Grigson rather sniffily says in her 1982 book *Fruit* that she is always being asked for recipes to use up Victorias. Nobody, she says, ever needs a recipe to use up green-gages. And sadly it seems that Sussex cannot lay claim to the greengage either, even if the village of Firle proudly maintains the fact on its website. It seems more than likely that the French 'Reine Claude' plum was sent to England to Sir Thomas Gage's home at Hengrave Hall in Suffolk (Suffolk again!), rather than to the present Lord Gage's ancestors at Firle. It is said that the original labels identifying the trees were lost on the journey from France to England, so Sir Thomas's gardener merely labelled the trees as 'Green Gage'. Whatever the tree's English provenance, a relative of the original plum is planted in the Firle gardens today.

And you can buy excellent greengage jam (if the trees are yielding) up the road at Middle Farm Shop, part of the Firle estate.

A narrow belt of green sand runs across the county between the chalk to the south and the clay to the north and it's on this band that much of the fruit-growing of the county has taken place and still takes place today. Acres of the dessert Leveller gooseberry, famed for its sweet taste, were grown on these sandy soils around Newick in the late 19th and early 20th centuries and sent to London by train. Arthur Wood of Sheepgate Fruit Farm at Newick still grows a few Levellers through his farm shop 'for sentiment' but claims that few are grown in the area now; other varieties are less demanding to grow and not so fussy as to soil type. The land that grew the Levellers has mostly gone for housing.

Further east, but on this similar light, sandy soil, Graham Love grows 45 acres (18 ha) of apples, pears, cherries and plums at his farm north of Herstmonceux. Love grows fruit for both supermarkets and local markets but is in no doubt as to which he prefers to supply – the people he sells to at farmers' markets around the county are just so much more appreciative, he says.

This is somewhat ironic, since Love is supplying them with technically 'inferior' fruit to the grade one fruit that he supplies to the leading supermarkets. Both sets of fruit may come from the same tree. The 'perfect' specimens (apples that are the right size, the right colour, and are free from even the tiniest blemish) will be sent to the supermarket. The apples that go to the farmers' market may not be so anatomically correct, but will have stayed on the tree a full two weeks longer than the supermarket fruit and be picked only the day before the market is held – so will be riper and juicier. It's that two weeks' extra maturity that makes all the difference to an apple's flavour. Love approached his local supermarket (an upmarket chain that champions its local connections) just three or four miles down the road, to propose that he run a few boxes of his apples to them a couple of times a week. The suggestion was greeted enthusiastically but the idea fizzled out when it was clear that the apples would still have to be delivered to the store's headquarters close to London in order to be shipped back to Sussex.

Love, who has spent the past 30 years responding to the different trends of the fruit market, sees his business moving away from supplying supermarkets (currently 80 per cent of his business) and towards a diverse operation of fruit and specialist vegetable growing, selling to local markets and greengrocers. A member of Transition Town Lewes, a community group formed 'to respond to the challenges of climate change and the end of cheap oil', he thinks it highly possible that in 20 years his farm will be one of several local producers supplying fruit to the Eastbourne area, just as happened a hundred years ago, as the industry moves away from nationally-structured supply chains to a far more local-based and less oil-dependent food economy.

Climate change is already affecting his farm, he says. The trend towards hotter summers means that it's now difficult to grow some traditional English apples like the Worcester in the south-east because the fruit starts to drop on the ground in the summer heat. However, the same increase in temperature means that he can now grow the late-maturing and good 'keeper' Braeburn that was difficult to grow here just 10 years ago. Varieties like the Cox are maturing three weeks' earlier than when his father bought the farm 55 years ago. Fruit is growing bigger, better and faster, Love says, maybe, he speculates, due to the very carbon dioxide emissions that we're all so worried about, carbon dioxide is what plants feed on, after all. However, warmer, wetter and greyer winters are likely to bring problems for fruit farmers in the south-eastern counties as the lack of ultraviolet from sunlight will be perfect for bacterial and fungal growth. Perfect for mushroom growing, though, he says with a grin.

PLUM TART

The secret of a good plum tart is to assess the sweetness of your chosen plums and adjust the glazing of the apricot jam. Ripe, sweet greengages will need only a swift glazing with a tablespoonful of hot apricot jam after the tart has baked. Bittersweet Victorias will need a generous five or six tablespoonfuls.

INGREDIENTS

- Shortcrust pastry made with 250 g of plain flour, 125 g of unsalted butter and a good pinch of salt
- Plums, between 20 and 30
- Caster sugar, 3–6 tablespoons, depending on taste
- Apricot jam, see above

INSTRUCTIONS

1. Preheat the oven to 190°C/ Gas Mark 5.

2. Line a 24-cm tart tin with the shortcrust pastry and put the tin in the freezer for five minutes to firm up after the rolling and handling. Line the tart case with baking parchment or foil, fill with baking beans or coins and bake the tart case 'blind' for around 15 minutes. Remove the beans and paper and put the tart back in the oven for two to three minutes so that the pastry loses its 'raw' look. Meanwhile, wash, dry, halve and stone the plums, discarding any pulpy ones. Taste one to judge its sweetness.

3. Remove the tart case from the oven and place it on a heat-proof mat. Now start to arrange the plum halves carefully in the case, cut side up, in concentric circles starting from the outer edge. Nestle the plums right up against each other as they will shrink a little during cooking – particularly the smaller greengages. Sprinkle the plums with between 3 and 6 tablespoons of sugar, depending on sweetness, and return the tin to the oven until the plums are tender – it will probably take around half an hour for the plums to get that swollen look and start to leach their juices onto the tart case. If the pastry looks like it's starting to burn, turn down the oven a little.

4. Take the cooked tart out of the oven and set it on a rack to cool. Heat the apricot jam in a saucepan until it starts to simmer. Sieve it into a bowl and either paint or spoon the jam over the tart.

5. Serve warm or cold.

VEGETABLES

BOX SCHEMES & ORGANICS

D rive around the Chichester bypass in the early spring and summer and you're likely to overtake at least one tractor. There's a high chance that it belongs to David Langmead – after all, he has 90 of them in the area. They all display a large number on the window of the front cab so that they're readily identifiable by the public. Any driving misdemeanour on the part of any one of the Langmead's staff, therefore, can be swiftly dealt with.

It's a small indication of the sheer size of this company and its concern to be seen to be doing the right thing. In 1986 Langmead took the decision to start to diversify his 1500 acres (600 ha) of wheat-based arable production when wheat dipped to a price he felt was unsustainably low. In his first year of horticultural business he harvested 80 acres of iceberg lettuces. Today the business occupies a total of 6500 acres (2600 ha) of land in the UK alone and the company harvests, amongst other crops, one and a half million conventionally-grown iceberg lettuces, 500,000 Romaine lettuces and 90 tonnes (100 tons) of baby leaf spinach each week. The figures are mind-boggling.

While most of the county copes with, and makes the best of, its poor terrain (Sussex contains some of the least productive land in England), much of the land on the south-coast flood plain between Brighton and Chichester is very high quality, being alluvial (river deposited) in nature. In addition, the area around Chichester has its own micro-climate; it sits in the Isle of Wight rain shadow which means that it has substantially less rain than, say Portsmouth, 15 minutes along the A27. So, with all these natural advantages, there's been a long history of intensive (by each century's own standards) arable and vegetable production in the area.

The Langmead season begins in February with planting on the most northern of the firm's farms near Petworth on the free-draining sandy soil of the area. As the season progresses, planting moves south to Oving, where the soil type is alluvial gravel. Every few weeks, the planting moves further south so that the latest crops of the year are sown right down by the coast and can benefit from the moisture-retentive, heavier soils. Here the temperature is two or three degrees higher and the quality of light is better. For every mile that the farm ventures inland, there is 10 per cent less light. The sky at the business's most southern farming location at Selsey has minimal cloud cover (it's no coincidence that the astronomer Patrick Moore has his home and observatory close by), so crops carry on growing consistently through the late summer season. When the season ends, production moves either to the firm's operations in Italy, or to its identical twin-sister business in southern Spain, so that salad production can be maintained year-round.

Organic farming makes up 20 per cent of the farm's turnover and because it depends far more heavily on crop rotation for disease-resistance than conventional farming, the choice of organic crops is wide – the land that has been sowed to baby leaf spinach one year can thus be sown to a brassica like cauliflower the next. Organic farming brings its own challenges to a farm so set up for efficient production schedules. The volumes of each crop are smaller, so labour operations are more complex. Rather than harvesting iceberg lettuce all day, for example, harvesting must change from one crop to another after only a couple of hours – different techniques, different packaging all takes time. And time, on a farm, where efficiency is king, where every trickle of irrigating water is measured and precision applied and where every iota of detail has been worked out to the nth degree, represents a great deal of money. Green waste, from both the wider community and the farm's own salad waste, provides the compost that replaces the artificial fertiliser that is applied on the conventionally-grown crops.

The company employs 128 full-time staff and 460 seasonal workers, mostly from eastern Europe. The seasonal workers are housed by the firm themselves – no outside agencies are employed, so that the company remains fully responsible for their employees' welfare. So rather than talk of 'gangmasters' and 'below the minimum wage', instead it's 'team barbecues' and 'English lessons'. But the rise in the standard of living of many of the new EU states and those states' ever-increasing expectations means that finding seasonal employees is getting progressively more difficult. The solution seems to be to try and mechanise their way out of using labour. Where once a lettuce was cut, crated, trailered to a packhouse, packaged, palleted and sent to be cooled, now it is cut, bagged, sealed, boxed, labelled, barcoded – all in the field where it grows. A process that once needed 36 people to get a lettuce into a cold store, can now be achieved with only 22.

Lettuce-growing East Sussex-style is on a much smaller basis. In contrast to the wide sweep of fine land to the west of the county, horticultural production in the east is mainly confined to pockets and thin strips of land sandwiched between the chalky Downs and the heavy clay soils of the Weald. A small island of this fertile sandy soil exists at Hankham, between Eastbourne and Polegate, witnessed by the sudden cluster of horticultural business here, now mainly growing flowering plants.

Hankham Organics is tucked away down a long track that suddenly opens out into a patch of land dominated by two great glasshouses, one of which, the largest in East Sussex, covers a staggering one and a half acres (0.6 ha) of fertile soil – a veritable cathedral of a structure. On a quiet Saturday afternoon it has something of the same hushed atmosphere. The long narrow beds that are set out grid-fashion in the house are filled with courgettes, aubergines, herbs and salad leaves. Ripening tomatoes hang down like strings of onions from the tall vines, thousands of pieces of carefully-tied blue twine suspended from the ceiling hold up the rows of tall pepper plants. All is neat and glossy – there's hardly a leaf out of place. A tall mass of ferny foliage bears witness to an earlier indoor asparagus harvest. There are beds of marigolds and borage 'to attract bees and other friendly insects' into the houses along with tall beds of amaranth grown for green manure to add fertility to the soil. Crops are rotated so that it's eight years before a particular plant will be grown again in the same area of the house, a practice that is vital to keep diseases like mosaic virus at bay.

Born in Brighton and attending school at Lewes (along with green-grocer Bill Collison of Bill's fame), Miles Denyer, the owner of Hankham Organics, worked for some 12 years in the horticultural industry. It was then that he realised that East Sussex was 'bad for organic vegetables', as he puts it, which rather neatly encapsulates his absolute conviction in the role of organic horticulture.

This is a very organic farm – not just in its dotted-line approach to biological pest control, say, or crop rotation, but in its holistic approach to every aspect of the way the business is run. The business uses no casual or foreign labour – just a dozen or more locals, which means, Denyer says, that 'we can pay them more and they can make a proper sustainable career out of the job'. There's no hierarchical structure to the firm – no farm manager telling people what to do. They are building a large and expensive underground tank for storing rainwater to help with the irrigation of the glasshouses. Denyer says quite frankly that he thinks that he will be 'in his seventies' before the tank pays itself, but it's simply 'a good green project' and therefore worth doing.

They have no plans to expand the business, he says, by moving into new areas because it's important to them that they keep their food miles low. Local really does mean local to them and that's the way it's going to stay, in contrast perhaps to other box schemes with nationwide ambitions. They operate in a small catchment area between Brighton and Eastbourne, delivering out 600 boxes a week but most of their customers are very close together so the food miles are kept very low. They also supply vegetables to other box schemes and shops, including a large amount of produce to Brighton-based Infinity Foods.

But organic aside, it's clear that Denyer is simply a dyed-in-the-wool horticultural farmer, passionate about soil quality, bemoaning the housing development that has taken place in the county as many do, but only because so much of it has taken place on the best agricultural land. And it seems a tragic waste to him that more horticulture isn't taking place in the eastern half of the county and that more farmers aren't entering this area of the industry. Most farmers would simply be pleased at the lack of competition.

The greengrocer

A year before the exceptional floods of October 2000 that left much of lowland Lewes under several feet of water, Bill Collison was expanding his shop. He employed three or four people and was negotiating with the shop next door so that he could expand the premises to include a café. Half of his business at the time was still the wholesale of fruit and vegetables. He was attracted to the greengrocery business initially, he claims, because he could finish work by lunchtime.

And then the autumn floods engulfed the town and his shop, situated almost on the bank of the river, was completely flooded out, as was Collison's home. The following day after the floodwater subsided he ran a makeshift market stall from the street in front of the shop. Although the business was 'underinsured' Collison says that the insurers behaved very well and it would be difficult to argue now that the floods didn't bring some long-term benefits to Cliffe High Street.

It's hard to imagine, looking at the shop today and its commanding position at the foot of the bridge, that it took months for the all-new Bill's Produce Store to take off; months when 30 staff were on the payroll and yet customers were scarce . For Bill's has become a retail phenomenon in the town – its café packed from early morning until closing time, a steady stream of customers stocking up either on greengrocery basics or bundles of asparagus. It's hard to think of a more enticing food shop – part café, part produce, where you eat amongst the food. Few greengrocers devote quite as much attention to the look of their shop; it's not unusual for Bill to be working on shop displays at three in the morning, arranging baskets and tubs. It's a cornucopia of fresh and grocery produce, where you have to heave your basket over bundles of flowers and trays of tarts in order to get to the till. The store's own van picks up fruit and veg from some of the shop's more local suppliers, and produce from the continent arrives via slow boat rather than aeroplane. Collison has opened a second shop and café (The Depot) in Brighton.

But perhaps the secret of Bill's in Lewes is that it feels like an institution in the town – its relaxed atmosphere makes it welcoming to all. Although the store doesn't officially open until eight in the morning, staff are there as early as five o'clock serving coffees to people on their way to work while the shop sets up for the day. And Collison is there more often than not, an eagle eye raking round the shop, a frown as he sees something not quite right, a cheery greeting to a regular. Never has buying a bag of apples in Sussex seemed more glamorous.

PART FIVE

BREAD & CAKES

I t is thought that one of the prime reasons for the Roman invasion of Britain had been southern England's already well-established wheat-growing regions. The Roman army needed ever larger supplies of wheat in order to control its growing empire, and the chalk uplands of the South Downs, easily cultivated with even the most primitive tools, must have been an attractive proposition. The Romans brought better tools, a wider variety of crops and probably more sophisticated working practices, so production intensified. The larger Roman villas discovered in the region tend to be concentrated in areas of prime arable land, as were, latterly, many of the county's landed estates – Cowdray, Petworth, Goodwood, Glynde and Firle. Agricultural rents were always traditionally much higher on the most productive land.

During the following 2000 years, arable cultivation across the county has risen and fallen, as market conditions like protectionism in wartime and free trade in peacetime have encouraged farmers to pick up or put down the plough. Historically, a high price for wheat – an expensive crop to grow in terms of labour, fertiliser and pesticides – has meant that many more of the county's acres have gone under the plough. When the price has dropped, due perhaps to the importation of corn from other countries or a sudden rise in costs, then land has reverted to grass, and the threshing machine and the combine harvester have returned to a dark corner of the barn or farm building.

BREAD

THE NEW BAKERS

Elizabeth David, in her 1977 book *English Bread And Yeast Cookery,* writes that the county of Sussex where she grew up had been a region with a reputation for 'good, sweet-eating bread'. She cites the reason for this being that many of the bakeries still had their own old-fashioned ovens and that Sussex was well-served by a network of mills – both wind and water – grinding up good, locally grown wheat grain. Several renovated mills across the county are still in working order today and occasionally grind corn, including both Polegate and Michelham Priory wind and water mills, close to David's childhood home at Wootton Manor, near Polegate.

The village bakery, the local mill – very few are left today across the county. By the time her book was published, David was bemoaning the passing of many of the traditional bakeries and highlighting the failings of their replacements. Much of the bread available now through supermarkets and the larger bakeries is produced by the Chorleywood Bread Process that was developed in 1961. The process relies on specialised machinery mixing the bread dough at high speed for around three minutes, moulding the bread into tins, proving the bread for about an hour and then baking it for 20 minutes. The high-speed mixing avoids the need for the slow fermentation of traditionally made bread and means that a loaf of bread can be made in under two hours. Hard fats and improvers have to be added to the dough in order for the process to be successful. Chorleywood was hailed in the 1960s as a way of providing cheap bread for the mass market – bread that would look very white, have a very even and regular crumb and would last a week. It was a triumph for the supermarket which could lure in customers with cheap, wrapped, keep-for-ever daily bread, but a disaster for the traditional family bakery.

We have sacrificed a great deal in terms of the quality of our bread simply to fit in with the commercial imperatives of the largest bakeries and our own attraction for ever-cheaper food. Happily, there are a few bakers in the county who are determined to put good-quality bread back on the shop shelves. They face a whole series of challenges, not least convincing some customers used to buying a loaf of bread in the supermarket for around 20p that a hand-crafted loaf that has taken a skilled baker 24 hours to make is good value. Supermarkets often use bread as a loss-leaders – tempting customers into the shop with a ridiculously low-priced item, confident that the spend in other areas will justify the loss on that one product. Good bakers are at a huge disadvantage in that the most expensive ingredient in a good loaf of bread is one that they can't readily put on the label – time.

In 2005, the co-founders of Green and Black's chocolate, Craig Sams and Jo Fairley, bought Judge's Bakery in Old Town's High Street, in Hastings, with the money that they made from selling Green and Black's to Cadbury's. The bakery business is not new to Sams – in the early 1970s he founded Ceres Bakery in London's Notting Hill which ran successfully for several years until it was badly hit, Sams says, by the newly elected Labour Government's decision to combat inflation by fixing the price of bread.

The couple had bought a house in Hastings after deciding to move away from London when their landlord died and they needed to get a foot on the property ladder. They chose Hastings for its sunny weather and because they liked the feel of the Old Town area – a little reminiscent of the Portobello Road that they had known in the 1960s, perhaps. Sams was working on his allotment just outside the town when a fellow toiler mentioned that he thought the High Street bakery was looking for a buyer. The baker agreed to sell and the new bakery, with the same name but a very different kind of operation, opened in Easter 2005, primarily selling bread but also a range of vegetables, dairy products and delicatessen items – all organic.

The old Judge's Bakery had been dependent on packet mixes for many of its products. Sams brought in baker Emanuel Hadjandreou who had previously worked, along with his wife, Lisa Sapire, at the high-profile Daylesford Farm shop in Oxfordshire, and also for Gordon Ramsay. Sams had met Hadjandreou some time earlier and had expressed his desire then to run a 'slow bakery'.

The aim of the bakery has been to raise the quality of the bread without alienating the traditional customer base so that the same sorts of breads appear on the shelves – the white sandwich loaves, the farmhouses and wholemeal tins – but instead made with organic flour and made properly in the traditional manner, without the use of improvers. The bakery does everything that a 'conventional bakery' does – sausage rolls (with organic pork) and white tin loaves, and even the old bakery's pink meringues have stayed in the shop, although now they're made with organic egg whites and tinted with natural food colourings like beetroot. But alongside the everyday familiar loaves which are priced relatively cheaply, the bakery sells sourdough loaves, ciabattas, ryes and other long-fermentation breads – priced more 'realistically'.

Sams rails at the industrialisation of bread, rating it far worse than what has been done to chocolate or wine, say. The over-yeasty, quickly made breads of the supermarket shelves, he claims, have given rise to the increase in coeliac disease, candida, and gluten intolerance. Not only has the flavour gone out of bread in the past 50 years, but its digestibility has reduced, and that's a high price to pay, he feels, to save a few pennies on a loaf.

The bakery supplies several local restaurants in the area . At the moment he's working on a formula for a franchise operation – supplying Judge's bread either baked, or part-baked and frozen for baking off in the franchisee's premises. This would allow the Hastings operation to keep control of the quality of the bread sold but liberate them from the sheer grind involved in starting up further shops themselves. Staffing in bakeries is always a major problem, Sams says. Such a high level of skill is involved in the process that if a member of staff is off sick, there's a major panic to get bread on the shelves for 8.30 in the morning.

Alastair Gourlay's Real Patisserie in Brighton had its genesis in France as Gourlay sat eating his breakfast, produce of the local boulangerie, and wondered why he couldn't get anything as good to eat back home in Britain. Gourlay stayed in France, abandoning a degree in agriculture, apprenticed himself to a bakery in the south and earned his Chambre Professionnelle des Artisans Boulangers-Pâtissiers qualifications, and then worked in Paris for around three years at several bakeries including the well-regarded boulangerie-pâtisserie Couderc. His plan from the very beginning was to get the necessary skills to come back to England and open a series of shops.

He admires the egalité of the French approach to food and is keen to apply it to his business. Good food is not a class issue in France as it can be in England, he says. Respect for food there seeps down into all sectors of society, not just the well-off. And so he has set out to make good, properly made bread and cakes free from the ornate snobbery of many of the French-inspired patisserie shops that often open over here in England but cater just for an upmarket, well-heeled clientele. In the 10 years since he has been back from France he has opened two shops in Brighton – one close to Brighton station and the other near Brunswick Square on Western Road, the flagship store of the operation. The actual bakery is set on the ground floor of a small business estate off the London Road – on the ground floor because his pride-and-joy French 'setter' oven that bakes much of his bread weighs over three and a half tons. Unlike the hot air-blowing ovens employed in most modern bakeries, the setter oven is heated by a network of steam pipes and the bread is baked on the floor of the oven which gives each loaf its moist quality and good crust formation. Gourlay thinks that he will stop short of his initial French ambition to have four shops. Two plus a large wholesale business that sends his bread out beyond the city's boundaries is enough for the time being, he thinks. He worries aloud that this sounds lazy, before going off to work a night shift in the bakery.

East West Bakery in Arundel is a family bakery in every sense of the word, although one that, unusually, revolves around the skills of the youngest members of the family. Bakers are 20-year-old brother and sister, Jenny and Sean Tennyson. Mother Sue handles the accounts and paperwork side of the business and father Guy acts as delivery driver and engineer. Older sister Laura makes the cakes. Sean and Jenny were first inspired to start making good bread while they were visiting Denmark and were amazed by the quality of the bakeries there. But it was a three-day course at Paul Merry's baking school at Shaftesbury in Dorset where they made a vast array of different sorts of bread and really studied the science of baking that was the real turning point for the project. They spent the next few months touring bakeries around the country and working with established bakers in Cornwall and Surrey.

After a lot of footwork they took on the lease of a bread shop in Arundel that had closed down, and from which they bought their baking equipment, as well as finding baking premises on a light industrial estate close to their home. One of the major difficulties was finding a baker to help them with the complicated logistical planning skills necessary for getting an array of different breads (all made from scratch with completely different doughs) ready for shop opening at 9 am every morning. Eventually the family sourced a Polish baker via a London agency. It seems that many of the new wave of bakeries opening now around the country are reliant on foreign expertise, so degraded have our own baking skills become.

The shop opened quietly in March 2007. The Tennysons stock a range of loaves – from traditional white farmhouses and London bloomers to apricot and walnut, and 100 per cent spelt loaves. All the breads are made slowly from Shipton Mill organic flour in the traditional manner from wheat or rye starters but one, the white sourdough, relies solely on wild yeast for fermentation. Plans are afoot to create a range of patisserie.

SUSSEX LARDY JOHNS

This is Samuelson's recipe for these little cakes. Make her 'sprinkling' of currants a generous one.

INGREDIENTS
MAKES AROUND A DOZEN

- *Flour, ¼ lb*
- *Lard, 2 oz*
- *Baking powder, ¾ teaspoonful*
- *Sugar, 2 teaspoonfuls*
- *Sprinkling of currants*

Rub all together in your hands, and add enough water to make a stiff paste. Cut the paste into squares and bake for about 10 minutes.

Sussex lardy cakes

Looking back to a tea-time era before the ubiquitous chocolate cake, it seems that the south-east isn't, by and large, famed for being a high-quality baking area. Few people could name a Sussex cake in the way that they could readily identify a Bath Bun or Eccles Cake. It seems that as one approaches the south-east our traditional cake-making tends towards the ultra-humble – we are in the land of the flead cake.

For a county without a notable pig-keeping tradition or even a native breed of pig, it seems strange that so many of the surviving Sussex recipes involve quite so much lard. But these recipes probably originate from a time when many households kept a pig or two in a sty at the bottom of the garden. A large supply of lard (rendered pig fat) would then have been readily available all through the winter months following the traditional pig-killing time in the late autumn as the weather chilled. For many perhaps, today's fat of choice, butter, would have been more of a summer option, made when milk was more plentiful.

M.K. Samuelson, in her fascinating *Sussex Recipe Book*, includes several 'lardy' cakes that are, on the whole, variations on an original theme, being all dough, fat and dried fruit. Unlike most cakes, where the fat plays an important but relatively subtle role, lardy cakes are, quite frankly, all about the lard, and whether you like them or not is absolutely dependent on your fondness for this fat.

Samuelson's recipe for Sussex Plum Heavies consists of bread dough kneaded through with lard, sugar and currants then formed into little buns. Other Sussex lard cakes involved rubbing the lard into flour (as if making pastry) and the resulting mix blended with sugar and dried fruit to make little cakes. Sussex Lardy Johns, Coger-cakes and Scrap Cakes are all based on this technique, though Scrap Cakes differ slightly in that the lard used is specifically the harder scraps of fat left over from the rendering of the fat. But all three of these recipes are, in essence, scones, and some of them (dense as they seem to turn out) probably originate from the time before the mid-19th century when Mr Bird invented his baking powder.

To my mind, cakes made with lard have definitely more appeal in the colder months of the year than in the heat of summer when soft lard fat turns to liquid grease at the merest touch of a warm hand. These are cakes as necessary suste-nance for a hard day's graft in the great outdoors. They're certainly a million miles away from the more usual dainty sponge of today's – occasional – tea table. And I'm afraid that, after a week of baking them, I have to say hooray for chocolate cake.

PART SIX

CHOCOLATE, HONEY
& PUDDINGS

Not so very long ago it was common to hear stories told of just how limited an array of sweet things was available to the rural population of Sussex. Family tradition has it, for example, that my husband's grandfather, who farmed in the Ouse Valley between Lewes and Newhaven, ate apple pie (after roast lamb) every day of his married life. Maybe his diet was simply a result of his wife's limited cooking skills, of course, but with apples in the orchard, wheat from his fields and butter and cream in the dairy it's easy to understand his reluctance to try something else.

But the range of delicious sweet treats produced in the county has improved enormously in recent decades. Largely gone are the traditions associated with the more challenging aspects of the county's reputation as seemingly the world centre of suet and dried fruit cuisine. Instead, Sussex is now rich in everything from pioneering chocolatiers to inventive chefs responsible for the creation of, among other things, the now world-famous Banoffi Pie.

CHOCOLATE-MAKING

A NOVEL SPECIALITY

There used to be two sorts of chocolate-makers – some very big companies producing mass-market chocolate sold in pennies-worth, and some very exclusive companies selling chocolates in gloves. There was the cheap treat and the expensive treat and there was not much in-between. But the emergence of 'middle-class' chocolate over the past 10 years has seen a fundamental shift in our chocolate-buying. We now mutter about cocoa percentages and single estates. Blocks of chocolate used to be simply dark, milk or white. Now they come flavoured with cardamom or chilli, ginger or even salt.

The processing of cacao beans is a highly industrialised affair and smaller chocolate makers in this country rely on supplies of couverture from specialist chocolate processors in northern Europe, usually Belgium. This couverture then has to be carefully tempered (precisely heated, stirred and cooled) so that the chocolate develops the correct smoothness and 'snap' and then the chocolatiers can exercise the full range of their talent – creating fillings and flavourings, moulding choco-late into intricate shapes and, almost as important, wrapping their chocolate into pleasing packaging that reflects just the right level of luxury for their chosen market.

There seems to be a disproportionately large number of companies making fine-quality chocolate in Sussex. Based almost entirely in the western half of the county, there's no discernible reason for this geo-graphical cluster, although it's fair to say that the founders of more than one company have stressed their ennui with London as a prime reason for settling out of the capital, albeit within striking distance of it.

It was a trip to Belgium's chocolate-making centre at Bruges that was inspiring to one set of West Sussex chocolate-makers. Chocolate Alchemists' co-founders Caroline Pring and Paul Leach were surprised to find the range of chocolate there so very boring and 'samey'. Going from shop to shop it was a case of 'yet more bloody Belgian seashells. We felt we could do better.' The company's aim is to bring chocolate into the 21st century, to create organic, high-quality, environmentally friendly, fair-trade chocolate and above all to make it fun. Three large and mesmerising tempering machines warm and stir white, milk and dark chocolate couverture, the starting point for their flavoured chocolate discs, their dark, white and milk slabs crusted with fruits and nuts and their bars stuffed with blackcurrants or flavoured with chilli. There are chocolate alphabet letters for children, as well as bundles of chocolate owls, frogs and rats specially made to coincide with the launch of the last book about You Know Who. Harrods, Selfridges and John Lewis sell their striking Easter eggs, simply yet effectively decorated with contrasting chocolate swirls and starbursts, beautifully packaged in coloured cellophane – it comes as no surprise that Pring has an art-college background.

The firm operates in converted stables in the appropriately chocolate-box village of Lodsworth on the Cowdray Estate and they prepare in July for the run up to Christmas – there will be no staff holidays until after Easter, just a lot of 18-hour days. With one shop established over the border in Guildford and two more planned (at the time of writing) they are increasingly cramped for space and are planning an extension.

Not so far away, Rory and Sarah Payne's chocolate company Cocoa Loco operates from their home near Horsham. The business started in 2005 when Sarah Payne started selling chocolate brownies from her kitchen on e-Bay after their youngest child had started school. Feedback – so central to the e-Bay business – was always extremely positive and orders flooded in, so much so that she was too busy baking to keep up with the accounts side of the business. At this point, Rory Payne gave up his own job in the foreign exchange department of a multinational bank. It was a daunting decision indeed, weighing up the benefits of abandoning long hours of commuting and having more time with his family, yet in the process giving up secure family-supporting employment.

The couple set up their own website with a mail-order shopping cart, selling brownies in gift boxes – they currently produce around eight different flavours, including chilli and coconut. Truffles followed shortly afterwards including a milk chocolate truffle with an orange, hazelnut and white-rum centre. The firm also produces mendiants – discs of chocolate loaded with dried fruit and nuts, as well as cookies, made to an old family recipe, and jumbo chocolate buttons. Some of these are definitely not for children – flavoured as they are with the ferociously hot Naga chilli. Inventiveness, sadly, has sometimes to be tempered with a pragmatic approach as to what is practical and affordable – a 'simply gorgeous' meringue flavoured with chocolate flakes had to be abandoned because it was 'an absolute bugger to make', and a cherry brownie had to go when the price of organic cherries became prohibitively expensive.

This reliance on sourcing organic products wherever possible is absolutely central to the company's philosophy, as is their commitment to good environmental practice. Their fair trade organic chocolate comes from the Dominican Republic, their eggs are sourced from a local organic farm and their dry ingredients come from Brighton-based wholefood suppliers, Infinity Foods. They've even tracked down a source of re-cycled aluminium foil, which naturally they reuse and recycle themselves.

Far from the West Sussex rural idyll, Anthony Heurtier makes exquisitely flavoured, entirely organic chocolates out of a small unit in a Brighton business centre that, even on a week-day afternoon, feels like a set for a gritty London gangster movie – you expect a gun-toting Michael Caine to come sprinting around the corridor at any moment. Heurtier came to Sussex without a word of English after working in pâtisseries in Brittany and Paris. He immediately found a job working for Alastair Gourlay's Real Patisserie and while working there set up his own company The Chocolate Empire in the autumn of 2006. He uses herbs, spices and essential oils to flavour his single-origin chocolate, sourced from either Peru or the Dominican Republic. White chocolate with cranberry and ylang ylang is a current flavour and he has developed a line of dark chocolate-covered maple fudge. Heurtier's Empire is small which makes it flexible enough to create chocolates with a short shelf life – many are filled with fresh cream. He also creates chocolates to order.

In fact, Brighton is a particularly 'chocolatey' town, the city's bohemian atmosphere supporting a diverse range of chocolate companies, ranging from tiny firms processing their own cocoa beans for 'raw' chocolate (no sugar and no milk products and, some might say, no discernible appeal), to larger companies with nationwide ambitions, and everything in between. Montezuma's opened its first chocolate shop in Brighton in August 2001. Only a couple of months earlier its co-founders Helen and Simon Pattinson had planned the shop merely as a retail outlet for a carefully selected chocolate maker that they had approached. But with just eight weeks to go before the shop was due to open, they put a call through to their proposed supplier only to get a bald little message on the answerphone to the effect that he had gone out of business. This was, as Helen Pattinson admits, a scary moment.

Both Pattinsons had held lucrative jobs in City law firms but disillusionment with the London rat race 'stepping out of the Tube on day one' meant that after four years, in 1999, they handed in their prospective notices, sold their home, put their furniture in storage and set off for South America with only the haziest of ideas of any plans for their longterm business future. As they backpacked their way from country to country, they kept diaries noting down any potential business ideas – at one time toying with the idea of setting up a company to import the milk-based syrup dulce de leche into Britain. But it was while they were staying in a little town, Bariloche, in the Argentine 'Lake District', that the Pattinsons had their first brush with the chocolate business. With Simon ill in bed with a stomach bug, Helen Pattinson wandered around the little town sampling exquisite chocolate from Bariloche's astonishing range of chocolate shops set up by an immigrant European population who had settled there after World War II. But the really defining moment came in Venezuela when they embarked on a long and arduous taxi journey from the coast into the hills, in the course of which they were constantly held up by cocoa farmers spreading their cocoa beans out on to the hot tarmac to dry. The Pattinsons ended up camping on a cocoa plantation and found out a lot more about the properties of 'such an amazing little tree'.

The South American tour came to an abrupt end when Simon Pattinson slipped a disc and the couple had to fly back to England the next day. While Simon recuperated on the floor, Helen Pattinson spent the next three months researching the viability of starting a retail enterprise selling high-quality, everyday chocolate that would bridge the gap between mass-market players like Cadbury's and the high luxury artisan end of the market. The business plan was formed, a suitable chocolate supplier found, a lease on just the right site in Brighton signed up, and then, disaster – no chocolate maker, no chocolate.

Rather than turning tail and fleeing the whole venture, the Pattinsons decided to set up in production themselves – tempering, blending and flavouring their own chocolate. Production initially started in a converted tack room in a farm building, quickly moved to an old pig barn, then finaly settled in its present situation in an industrial unit. The cocoa beans for their chocolate are sourced from selected growers in the Dominican Republic and the beans are processed in Belgium.

Pattinson admits that their lack of retail experience has caused problems at times – the opening of the shop was delayed by two days when they realised that they had no labels on the shelves that would identify the different chocolate bars for their customers. And she realises that they took a big risk opening their first shop in mid-August when customers are usually heading for the beach and a cold ice cream. But she believes that their inexperience has also been a strength of the business as it makes them closer to their customers. They still actively seek out employees without retail experience so that people come to the company with fresh ideas and a lack of perceived retail wisdom.

Across the road from Montezuma's, Choccywoccydoodah provides a complete contrast to the quiet elegance of its neighbour, making extravagant and extraordinary chocolate cakes of breathtaking detail. They specialise in chocolate sculpture and train their chocolatiers in the art of chocolate 'floristry'. Even if you're not in the market for a cake of such extravagance, it's worthwhile peering into the window of their shop in Brighton's Duke Street to puzzle at the gravity-defying construction of some of their cakes and wonder if this can truly be chocolate.

Honey

In *His Last Bow*, Sherlock Holmes retired to a farm on the Downs five miles from Eastbourne to write his magnum opus 'Practical Handbook of Bee Culture, with some observations upon the segregation of the Queen'. Surely the celebrated detective had done his homework and settled in the county best suited to the perusal of his study? Alas, it seems that Conan Doyle's choice of retirement location for Holmes was due to his own connections with the county rather than any specific bee-keeping culture. There are plenty of idiosyncrasies and superstitions in the bee world – the importance of going to tell the bees of a death in the family and draping the hives in black crêpe, for example, and each county's beekeepers tend to claim these sorts of stories as their own. But these are usually universal stories, common to bee-keepers not just in England but around the world.

With some notable exceptions like in the north of England where heather moorland has been, and still is, a feature of the terrain, honey elsewhere in the country has been largely multi-floral until comparatively recently. The big change in the past 30 years has been the widespread growth of oil-seed rape as part of an arable rotation of crops and the arable areas of Sussex have grown their fair share of the yellow-flowered plant. According to Billingshurst bee-keeper, Roger Patterson of the West Sussex Beekeepers Association, the first varieties of oil-seed rape that were grown flowered for eight weeks at a time. This caused a revolution in honey production – overnight a colony's yield jumped from around 30lb a season to closer to 100lbs. Modern oil-seed rape varieties now flower for only three to four weeks and so there has been a corresponding fall in colony production to around 60lb. Rape makes a fairly ordinary, everyday sort of honey that crystallizes very quickly. Pasture planted to clover makes for a better-regarded honey, and the bramble bushes that smother the Weald, given the chance, are a good source of blackberry nectar, but for most Sussex beekeepers summer honey is almost always a mixture.

SUSSEX PUDDINGS

SUET & TOFFEE

Few authors have published a book on English cookery over the past ten years that hasn't included a recipe for Sussex Pond Pudding, the suet crust pudding stuffed with sugar, butter and a whole lemon that, when cut open, oozes buttery, lemony, sugary juices – the 'pond'. But early recipes for Pond Pudding make no mention of the lemon – just the ball of butter and sugar and, to my mind, a pretty stodgy mixture it is too. The reputation for Sussex as a centre for suet cookery was such that it was said that to venture into the county was to risk being turned into a pudding yourself. And by pudding, we mean the full range of suet puddings, both sweet and savoury. Puddings might contain eels, partridges, bacon, rabbit or beef steak – probably whatever was to hand or cheap and plentiful. Florence White in *Good Things in England* says that puddings are made out of everything in Kent and East Sussex, just as pasties are made out of everything in Cornwall. Sussex Blanket Pudding was another boiled suet affair – a jam or golden syrup or mince-meat roly-poly.

But of course not all puddings are strictly 'puddings'. A Sussex version of apple pie was sweetened with a syrup made from simmering the cores and peelings of the apples with sugar and reducing this liquid down to just a few tablespoons of sweet juice. And when the pie was cooked, the lid was lifted and a custard of eggs and cream poured in.

Less traditional, but now found all over the world, Banoffi Pie can be absolutely located not just to Sussex but to one Sussex restaurant, the Hungry Monk in Jevington. Consisting of a cooked pastry base filled with toffee made from a well-boiled can of condensed milk, topped with sliced banana and coffee-flavoured cream, it's as filling to the 21st-century palate as the suet pudding was in the 18th century and even involves the immersion of an article in boiling water for three hours.

Sussex chef and 'creator' of Banoffi Pie, Ian Dowding, says that the pudding has its origins in a recipe brought back from America called 'Blum's Coffee Toffee Pie' and that making the toffee part of the pie was originally a tricky mixture of boiling sugar, butter and cream. It was while Dowding was working as head chef at the Monk that his sister told him about the practice of boiling cans of condensed milk to make toffee. Dowding realised that this would be the perfect way to make the pudding and so 'resurrected' the recipe. But it wasn't until a layer of sliced banana was added between the toffee and the cream that the pudding became Banoffi Pie. It has stayed on the restaurant menu ever since. One can only estimate how many kitchens across Sussex – across the world, even – have been redecorated following the boiling dry of a neglected can of condensed milk.

HONEY & GINGER ICE CREAM

A soft, creamy ice cream that doesn't need any attention once you've put it in the freezer. Serve with nutty little biscuits.

INGREDIENTS

- Honey, 3 tablespoons
- Ginger syrup from a jar of crystallised ginger, 3 tablespoons
- Double cream, 300 ml
- 3 egg yolks

1. Measure out the honey and the ginger syrup into a small saucepan and bring slowly to the boil, stirring from time to time. Meanwhile, separate the eggs and put the yolks into a freestanding mixer with a whisk attachment.

2. When the syrup boils, switch on the mixer to high speed and pour the very hot syrup in a thin stream into the whisking egg yolks. Mix for around five minutes or until you have a thick creamy mixture. Gently whisk in the double cream until thoroughly blended, pour the mixture into a plastic box and place in the freezer until firm. Eat within 48 hours.

PART SEVEN

BEER, CIDER & WINE

Commercial English winemaking is at last emerging from its long adolescence into promising maturity. The county's winemakers, benefiting from a greater pool of expertise and a general pattern of kinder summers, are at the forefront of what finally feels like the beginnings of a proper English wine industry. Sales of real cider are growing in the county – perhaps fuelled by some high-profile advertising by a national cidermaker – but fuelled nonetheless, and this in a county where cider has never been widely made. It's beer that's long been the drink of choice in Sussex – hops and barley being traditionally grown extensively right across the county. But sales of real ale have fallen country-wide over the past 30 years as national and multinational breweries have taken an ever greater hold of the market. The number of brewers may have fallen sharply in Sussex over the past century (Lewes alone once had half a dozen or so different breweries), but the county's remaining brewers both large and small still inspire the kind of loyalty that is rarely found amongst consumers.

BEER

THE COUNTY DRINK

Sussex was for a long time the second most important hop-producing county in the country – second only to Kent – so it's not surprising that Sussex beers have traditionally been quite bitter and hoppy in character. Production of the herb was focused mainly on the eastern High Weald and was traditionally linked in with cattle farming. The past 20 years have seen big changes in the Sussex brewing scene as old established brewers have disappeared into the ether and new start-ups have appeared on the scene. There are currently around 20 breweries in the county, ranging in size from mainly cask ale manufacturers like Harveys, with its estate of more than 40 tied houses, to much smaller bottled beer operations and pub breweries.

Harveys

The year 2000 was a traumatic one for the beer industry in Sussex. In the west of the county there were shockwaves as the highly respected brewery, King and Barnes, was sold to a Dorset company, Hall and Woodhouse. And just six months later in the east of the county, heavy rain and high tides caused the River Ouse in Lewes to burst its banks and flood the lower-lying areas of the town. Harveys brewery, nestled against the riverbank, disappeared under several feet of water in mid-brew. Before the evacuation of the brewery took place, a last-minute decision was made to cut short the usual brewing process and add the yeast to the fermenting vessel even though it contained only the very strongest worts. The subsequent ale, with its 6.5 per cent alcohol content, came quickly to be known as 'Ooze Booze'. The beer was tankered to a Kent brewery, Shepherd Neame, for bottling and Ooze Booze became a run-away bestseller, mentioned in the national press and radio, the proceeds going to the Lewes Floods Appeal.

Miles Jenner, head brewer and joint managing director at Harveys, doesn't want to see the brewery's beers sold outside a 50-mile (80-km) limit. If you could buy a Harveys ale anywhere in the country, he reasons, why would you go out of your way to buy it in Sussex? 'Besides, beer is 90 per cent water, and it seems silly to transport water from one region to another.' So rather than dream of national celebrity, the company concentrates on its Sussex identity and heritage, highlighting local history and even saying its thankyous with the launch of various seasonal and special ales. Knots of May, for instance, appears with the start of the Morris Dancing season and was first brewed to celebrate the local group's 21st birthday. Bonfire Boy is brewed every autumn for the November bonfire season although it was originally called Firecracker and was created as a tribute to the emergency services who assisted the firm when the brewery shop caught fire in 1996. And calling a bottled beer after Thomas Paine, who lived in Lewes before heading off to write revolutionary propaganda in aid of the American War of Independence, is a shrewd choice for a town with a somewhat radical character itself.

That radical character showed itself strongly in 2007 when stalwart Harveys drinkers revolted against Greene King's decision to withdraw Harveys from Greene King's own Lewes Arms pub. A mass boycott, boosted by national and even international press coverage, led to the bigger brewery's climbdown.

Harveys' bestselling and flagship beer is its Sussex Best Bitter, created in the 1950s as a post-rationing response to the weaker wartime beers. The same spring has supplied the water for the brewery for well over a century, and the same yeast strain has been in continuous use now for 50 years. Hops for the beers are sourced from Sussex, Kent and Surrey in roughly equal proportions to the beer's distribution. Barley, though, comes from East Anglia where the maltster is situated as there doesn't seem to be much point, Jenner says pragmatically, in hauling barley to a maltster and then bringing it all the way back to Sussex again. The spent grain is carried on Harveys' liveried trailers to the local agricultural college at Plumpton for cattle feed so that even the brewery's waste products trundle through the town, a source of local pride.

Hepworth

A chapter of Horsham's brewing history came to an abrupt end in 2000 with the closure of the town's King and Barnes brewery. Situated close to the town centre, the real estate of the brewery had become so valuable that the decision was taken by shareholders to sell the brewing operations to Hall and Woodhouse and the land for development.

The core of King and Barnes' old production team – head brewer Andy Hepworth, bottle manager Tim Goacher, chief engineer John Tewson and brewer Paul Webb – formed a new company, Hepworth & Co, on the site of an old weedkiller factory next to the railway lines in the town. The plan was to capitalise on their combined experience and established reputation in the brewing world and start a large brewery business, concentrating most of the brewery production on bottled ales and lagers.

The largest part of the Hepworth business is conditioning and packing beers for other brewers. Production is very flexible and can be quickly changed from day to day to deal with different beers for different companies. But Hepworth also brews its own beers including a classic ale, Pullman, and Sussex, which is made from locally-grown barley from Chichester and hops from Bodiam. This beer carries the newly-created 'Warranty of Origin' label – an English version of the *Appellation d'Origine Côntrolée* mark, adopted by the French for each of their wine appellations – which guarantees the local provenance of a beer's ingredients. Hepworth's own organic lager and its biggest seller, Blonde, is grown with English barley and Belgian hops, it being difficult to source a quality supply of organic home-grown hops at present. Only a fifth of what the firm bottles is currently its own brewed product although the plan is to increase this shortly to 50 per cent.

The firm also specialises in beer development, supplying a major brewery, say, with a recipe and design package for a new lager. And the firm is flexible enough to take on smaller contracts too. Last year, Hepworths developed a lager for the Goodwood Estate using the estate's own malting barley for sale in the estate's hotel, farm shop, and the bars and restaurants connected to its racing circuit and racetrack.

Fallen Angel

According to Tony and Gaby Betts, husband-and-wife brewers from Battle, there's a disproportionate number of IT specialists involved in the brewing industry. Apparently the skills are much the same – they have to be as methodical and analytical in their brewing career as they ever were when they were servicing computer systems. They initially started by making beer in casks but moved over to bottled beer so as not to compete with the existing market of the vast majority of brewers in the area. Their first brewery must have been the only garage in Battle to be licensed by the police and customs and excise.

They took a long time choosing the right name for the brewery, finally settling on Fallen Angel, a name suited to the kind of beers that they were wanting to create – a mixture of the traditional and the modern. There's nothing traditional about the labels, though. Around half feature a variety of scantily clad women in compromising situations drawn by erotic artist Lynn Paula Russell.

The labels may be an important marketing tool, but ultimately it's the content of the bottles that really matters and Fallen Angel has a loyal following. Production has doubled over the past six months since they moved to bigger premises on the outskirts of Battle and the company regularly brews 18 different beers. This is too many, Gaby Betts maintains, but every time they try to end a line, a flood of requests keeps it in production. The selection is wide – from the hoppy Gamekeeper's Bitter to the robust darkness of St Patrick's Irish Stout. A chilli-flavoured beer initially trialled just for 'a bit of a joke' has become a runaway bestseller, so much so that the Betts responded to the demand for a hotter ale with Black Death, brewed using the ferocious Naga chilli.

While the Betts may have no qualms about the diversity of ingredients they use in their beers, they use no chemicals or finings, preferring the beers to clear naturally. Company policy is not to supply the beer to chains of shops and for only one shop per town to run the Fallen Angel stock – 'better for the shopkeepers', Tony Betts says. Fairs, shows and farmers' markets dominate the schedule and the Betts have no weekends free in the foreseeable future.

CIDER

CURATORS & MAVERICKS

Sussex may not now be famed for its cidermaking but it can boast the National Collection of Cider and Perry at Middle Farm, Firle. As Rod Marsh of Middle Farm admits, it's a distinct advantage to be in neutral territory if you're showcasing all the different ciders of the country. At first the cider collection was housed in a narrow corridor with only enough room for three people to taste and browse at any one time, but in 1990 the cider section moved to its own building and was immediately a huge success. It finally got its 'National Collection' designation from Companies House in 2003 by proving its pre-eminence in the field, and indeed there is nowhere like it.

Middle Farm now stocks over 200 different ciders made by 75 different cidermakers from all over England, including the Farm's own cider, Pookhill. At least once a week, Marsh sets off at 3.30 am to pick up cider from four or five different producers in a specific area, bringing back around 250 gallons at a time. Demand is so strong that he's keen to relocate the cider collection to a new, larger building on the farm so that they will have room to feature more international ciders. Freshly pressed juice is always available, and people with their own well-stocked apple trees can bring them in for pressing.

Sussex has less than a dozen or so 'above the parapet' cidermakers, and there's still a concentration of cidermaking expertise in the western half of the county. At Gospel Green, James and Cathy Lane make traditional champagne-method Sussex Cyder on the Sussex/Surrey border near Lurgashall. At Maplehurst, John Batcheldor presses cider apples for his JB cider on an ancient Sussex single-screw press which is over 100 years old.

Cidermakers, Marsh says affectionately, are all mavericks but Richard Jupp, who makes Wild Thing cider from a purpose-built shed at his home in Portslade, is more maverick than most. Jupp owns no orchards but, along with his brother, gathers his apples from trees on the Downs, on common land and abandoned orchards and along the roadsides in the Brighton, Haywards Heath and Lewes areas. He is understandably coy about exact locations although he seems to fear animal competition almost as much as human. Jupp has seen cows working in pairs – one rocking the tree with her back and the other scrabbling up the tree to snatch at the fruit. 'It's a particularly fine tree', he says, as if this explains the bovine acrobatics.

New opportunities emerge all the time. The trees that have been planted along new dual carriageways to muffle sound over the past 10 years often contain apple trees amongst them, he says, and they're now proving a useful source. He now gathers around 6 tonnes (7 tons) of apples a year between late August and late December, and makes around 250 gallons (950 litres) of cider. Many of the trees are 'wildings' – chance seedlings that have sprouted from a discarded core. He has even seen twin trunks emerging out of the ground, obviously from the same core, that bear apples of completely different types, usually in alternate years. He's had his share of bumps, scratches and falls over the years from splitting branches – these are not well-managed trees, after all, and is these days a little more circumspect about picking apples after a few early-morning encounters in the past 'dodging the traffic'.

He makes his cider without yeast in the old-fashioned way – he just mills the apples, presses the juice and fits an airlock to the fermenting jars. The cider is made in small batches as he gathers the apples, which he then blends together to make a pleasing combination. Sometimes two quite unpromising separate ciders can blend into a very drinkable cider. One huge tree he knows of yields apples like concrete but the high tannin content of the cider made from these apples may be just what another rather wishy-washy cider needs to perk it up. Despite the fact that his raw material changes constantly, his success is consistent – winning local awards for cider categories at the Sussex Beer Festival at Hove, and again at the Southdowns Beer Festival at Lewes.

WINE

PRIZE-WINNING VITICULTURE

Winemaking in England as a whole has had a sporadic history of development. It is likely that the Romans introduced quality winemaking to England, and that Roman vineyards were planted as far north as Leicestershire. Winemaking dwindled in the Viking era but became more popular with French cultural influence after the Norman Conquest. After the dissolution of the monasteries under Henry VIII there seems to have been a gradual decline in the number of vineyards, perhaps also due in part to the cooling of the climate during the Little Ice Age between 1600 and the mid-19th century. Commercial viticulture seems to have ceased in England completely between the two World Wars.

With the first commercial modern vineyard in England only established in the mid-1950s (over the border in Hampshire), English winemakers have not had the advantage of an unbroken run of tradition that their counterparts across the Channel have had. Starting up a vineyard and making wine is a highly capital-intensive business – land to buy, vines to plant, expensive processing machinery to finance – and it's some six or seven years before a new vineyard can expect to see any return on such a big investment. But a growing skillbase and an upwardly mobile summer temperature has meant that Sussex winemakers are at the forefront of a revolution that now puts several of the county's wines into serious contention with some of the highest-quality wines produced across the Channel.

A wide variety of wines are made in the county – from dry crisp whites, to fruity reds and traditional-method sparkling wines, both white and rosé. Winemaker Peter Hall, at Breaky Bottom near Lewes, has weathered the vagaries of winemaking since 1974, producing flowery German-style whites and, more recently, Chardonnay-based sparkling wines. While English wine makers are – at present at any rate! – unable to make the heavy red wines that come from the hotter southern European vineyards, fine fruity English reds are more than possible. Bookers Vineyard at Bolney has won acclaim for its Dark Harvest wine made from a blend of the Rondo and Dornfelder grape varieties – full-bodied red wine grapes with dark, ruby red flesh that are early-ripening and so extremely suitable for our shorter summers.

Certain areas of Sussex share a remarkable similarity in soil type to that of the Champagne region of France – the South Downs lie less than 100 miles (160 km) north – and the general rise in summer temperatures over the past few years has allowed the region's winemakers to set their sights on varieties that would have been difficult, nigh impossible, to grow 20 years ago. The English mix of increasingly hot summer days and cool summer evenings helps to keep up the acidity levels which are ideal for making sparkling wine. Indeed, there are concerns in the Champagne area of France that the increasingly hotter climate there will have a long-term adverse effect on the quality of their wines. Rumours abound of vintage champagne houses from France crossing the Channel to eye up potential Sussex locations.

The two great enemies of viticulture in England are mildew and late frosts. At Ridgeview, north of Ditchling, mildew is controlled by careful weed control and general good crop management. Frost, though, is combated with a solution that is both high-tech and pleasingly eccentric. Between March and May, a weather station placed in the middle of the vineyard senses if the temperature is approaching the danger level of two degrees above zero and sends out an automatic text message to warn of the fact. At which point it's a high-speed charge to the vines for the Roberts family and the hand lighting (and later laborious extinguishing) of dozens of paraffin candles, placed in alternate rows – the fug created is enough to keep the temperature above the danger level.

Surely it's this attention to detail and their insistence on doing everything just right that has been the secret to Ridgeview's phenomenal success as a producer of outstanding English sparkling wine. Their first small harvest of grapes in 1996 for their Bloomsbury wine earned them the accolade of English Wine of the Year. Countless awards have followed – 'we like to enter competitions' – and their wine was chosen for the Great British Menu for the Queen's 80th birthday celebrations in 2006.

Ridgeview was founded when Michael and Christine Roberts sold their computer hardware and software business in 1993 and, keen winelovers, they decided to start making wine. After initially flirting with the idea of buying a vineyard in France, they settled for making fine sparkling wine in Sussex instead, buying the land in Ditchling later that year. The vines were planted in 1994, and the couple studied at Plumpton College, which runs the only courses dedicated to viticulture and oenology in the country. The vineyard is a true family affair – the Roberts are joined by their son, Simon, who runs the day-to-day wine-making, and their daughter Tamara who, with a background in finance, works as general manager. Their daughter-in-law, Mardi, takes care of marketing and sales.

Ridgeview is run on the lines of a premium Champagne vineyard but with a little New World practicality thrown in. Vines are tended so that the grape clusters that grow horizontally above the main bough are located at waist rather than knee height – the tradition in most French vineyards – apparently it's much easier on the back. But the grapes are treated with all due reverence – the vines are pruned hard because quality not quantity is the order of the day and the pickers, mostly regulars, who come to hand-harvest the grapes are instructed to handle them as if they were as fragile as light bulbs. Three grape varieties are grown – Chardonnay, Pinot Noir, and Pinot Meunier – all classic 'Champagne' grapes.

Once pressed, the juice is racked after a night's rest and the yeast is added – the grape varieties remain in separate tanks at this point. Fermentation takes two weeks and then the young wine remains in the tank for six to nine months while a further malolactic fermentation takes place which softens the acid nature of the wine. The wines are then blended as desired (or not, as in the case of Ridgeview's pure Chardonnay Grosvenor wine), filtered and a second amount of yeast is added along with sugar before bottling. At this stage, a small plastic 'trap' is inserted under the metal beer-style cap to capture the sediment that will form in the bottle. The bottles are stored flat for the next 18 months in the capacious temperature-controlled cellars beneath the winery. 250,000 bottles can be stored here but with three years' worth of wine needing to be stored the Roberts have plans for an extension to their cellar storage. Then the bottles are 'riddled', or mechanically jolted and tilted, until they are fully upside down so that the sediment in each bottle settles in the plastic trap. At this point the neck of each bottle is frozen, and the frozen plug of sediment removed from the wine. A little sugar is added and the wine is corked, wired and labelled. The whole winemaking process at Ditchling mirrors the 'traditional method' of the French Champagne winemakers.

Ridgeview wines are all sold under the Merret trademark and named after areas of London – suitably upmarket ones, of course. Christopher Merret was a 17th-century Londoner who first detailed the manufacture of sparkling wine in London some 30 years before the French are known to have made sparkling wine. Roberts cherishes a long-term ambition that the Merret name will one day be a generic name for English sparkling wine, just as cava is to Spanish, and prosecco to Italian.

Demand for the company's wines has been such that, at the time of writing, callers at the vineyard are restricted to purchasing just one bottle each. So it's reassuring that the Roberts anticipate a five-fold increase in production over the next 10 years as they expand the number of vines under cultivation.

Acknowledgements

Fizz Carr would like to thank the following for their assistance:

Matthew Berryman, Francis Brand, John Craig, Lord Gage, David Guy, Jim Harrison, John Harvey, Richard Johnson, Hilary Knight, Jane Nash, Roger Patterson, Stephen Potter, Eleanor & David Robins, Camilla Thelandersson, Roger Waters and Andy Weller.

FESTIVALS &
FARMERS' MARKETS

Food festivals & fairs

BRIGHTON FOOD & DRINK FESTIVAL
Throughout September
www.brightonfoodfestival.co.uk

CHILLI FIESTA
West Dean Gardens
Annually in August
www.westdean.org

FEASTBOURNE
Eastbourne
Annually in October
www.feastbourne.com

GLYNDE FOOD & DRINK FESTIVAL
(Now incorporating the English
Wine Festival)
Held in September
www.glynde.co.uk

HASTINGS SEAFOOD & WINE FESTIVAL
Annually mid-September
www.visit1066country.com/events

RYE SCALLOP FESTIVAL
Annually in February
Around a dozen local restaurants put
Rye's favourite bivalve on the menu,
giving us all the chance to gorge on
this local delicacy.

Farmers' markets

ARUNDEL Monthly, 3rd Saturday
BATTLE Monthly, 3rd Saturday
BEXHILL Monthly, 4th Thursday
BREDE Every Friday
BRIGHTON & HOVE
    Monthly, 1st Sunday
BURGESS HILL Monthly, 2nd Thursday
CHICHESTER
    Monthly, 1st & 3rd Friday
CROWBOROUGH
    Monthly, 4th Saturday
EAST DEAN Every Wednesday
EAST GRINSTEAD
    Monthly, 1st & 3rd Thursday
FIRLE Monthly, 4th Sunday
FORD Monthly, 1st Saturday
HAILSHAM Monthly, 2nd Saturday
HASTINGS
    Monthly, 2nd & 4th Thursday
HAYWARDS HEATH
    Monthly, 4th Thursday
HEATHFIELD Monthly, 3rd Saturday
HORSHAM Every Saturday
HOVE Monthly, 4th Saturday
LEWES Monthly, 1st Saturday
MIDHURST Monthly, 4th Saturday
PETWORTH Bi-monthly, 4th Saturday
RYE Every Wednesday
UCKFIELD Monthly, 1st Saturday

INDEX